TOBIAS AND THE ANGEL

Theatre editions of James Bridie's plays uniform with this volume

The Anatomist

Babes in the Wood

Daphne Laureola

Dr. Angelus

Jonah and the Whale

King of Nowhere

The Last Trump

Mary Read
(with Claud Gurney)

Mr. Gillie

The Queen's Comedy

A Sleeping Clergyman

Susannah and the Elders

The Switchback

TOBIAS AND THE ANGEL

by

JAMES BRIDIE

With an Introduction and Notes
by A. C. WARD

LONDON
CONSTABLE & CO LTD

LONDON

PUBLISHED BY

Constable and Company Ltd
10 *Orange Street, W.C.2*

First published . . . . . (*in one volume with two other plays*)	1931
First published in separate form . .	1931
Second Edition, revised . . .	1932
Reprinted twenty-eight times between 1933 *and*	1960
Third Edition with Introduction and Notes	1961
Reprinted	1966
Reprinted twice	1967
Reprinted three times . . .	1968
Reprinted	1969

SBN 09 452810 1

PRINTED IN GREAT BRITAIN BY OFFSET LITHOGRAPHY BY
THE ANCHOR PRESS LTD., TIPTREE, ESSEX

TO J. D. M. RORKE

Character costumes and wigs used in the performance of plays contained in French's Acting Edition may be obtained from Messrs. Charles H. Fox, Ltd., 184 High Holborn, London, W.C.1

The incidental music for this play is published by Messrs. Samuel French, Ltd., price 2s. 0d. per copy.

AUTHOR'S NOTE

THIS play is a plain-sailing dramatic transcription of the charming old tale told in the Book of Tobit in the Apocrypha.

One or two liberties have been taken with the text. The language spoken by the characters has been altered from a rather portentous Jacobean phraseology to a speech belonging to no particular period—a speech that might equally have been used by a pupil of Swift or an apostle of Arnold Bennett. The opinions of the characters are substantially unaltered, except those of Sara. It seemed natural that she should fall in love with her supernatural Tristan, and equally natural that, like a sensible girl, she should accept the inevitable.

I thought it necessary, too, that an Archangel, for whom time had no objective reality, should be a thorough Modern. He has, therefore, stolen a little from a vague recollection of Plato's dialogues. Apart from this, his detachment, his dignity and his peculiar sense of humour are all to be found in the original.

A certain characteristic of the Afreet, Asmodeus, is described in Reginald Scott.

J. B.

INTRODUCTION

By A. C. Ward

I

By writing plays in a modern and humorous manner about Scriptural characters, James Bridie was following though not consciously imitating a practice begun by English dramatists centuries ago. It may seem strange to say that those medieval dramatists were writing in a modern manner, but though they are medieval to us they were of course " modern " to themselves: they wrote the kind of language their audiences could understand easily and did not try to imitate in an English translation an old-fashioned " historical " style of speaking which they might have supposed was used by Noah and his family or by the shepherds watching their flocks at the time of Christ's birth.

Not only did those playwrights use their own contemporary language in their biblical dramas, they also introduced comic scenes and jokes which no doubt reminded the audiences of things happening in their own neighbourhood. In the play about the Flood, Noah's wife is a scold; in one of the Shepherds' plays there is a thief who tries to hide a sheep he has stolen by dressing it up and putting it into a baby's cot. Even though we do not know that Noah's wife really bullied her husband or that there were sheepstealers in Palestine, it is quite likely that both are true, and it is pretty certain that the medieval English audiences knew such persons among their own acquaintances and would enjoy seeing and hearing these characters shown up and made fun of.

We may think, however, that plays dealing with sacred themes should not have comic bits put into them; that these are religious matters and should be treated seriously. But such a view of religion is too narrow. It is uncomplimentary to the Creator to suppose that we are not intended to use all the good gifts with which we are born, one of the most precious of which is the gift of laughter. Religion does indeed treat of serious matters, but there is no sound reason for treating serious things as though they were solemn and dull. The medieval playwrights recognized that the religious lessons their plays were intended to teach could best be impressed by making the audiences enjoy what they were watching. And, in any case, those who wrote the plays were having fun, and they wanted others to have fun too.

When writing *Tobias and the Angel* and his plays about *Jonah and the Whale* and *Susannah and the Elders*, James Bridie was no doubt less concerned about giving Scripture lessons than the unnamed dramatists in the Middle Ages were. Their plays were intended to provide religious teaching for people who could not themselves read the Bible. Bridie wrote to provide entertainment, yet in *Tobias and the Angel* he managed to slip in a good deal of wisdom bearing upon good and sensible living. He himself wrote in his autobiography, *One Way of Living* (1939):

> *Tobias* and *Jonah* were about God and the relation of the individual man to Him. These tremendous themes I treated in the only manner I had at my disposal—the jocular conversational manner. Apart from the themes I had done everything I could to make the plays works of art. I used every trick I could find and a few I invented for myself. If the plays had been about nothing there would still have been something to have been said for them. They were neat and lively and kept the audience awake.

Since the first performance at Cambridge in 1930, *Tobias and the Angel* has become one of the best loved of modern plays, and a pleasing coincidence is that, like the medieval plays which were written to be played out of doors in public places, Tobias has been often performed with success at the Open Air Theatre in Regent's Park, London.

The true object of using modern idiom in a play about remote times is to save the audience from feeling cut off by strangeness of speech from close human contact with the characters. In a former type of conventional romantic novels and plays on historical subjects, authors tried to suggest a " sense of period " by introducing phrases and forms of speech supposed to have been used at the time; but the effect produced was hardly better than a sense of oddity which made readers and audiences think of the characters as strange creatures. Present-day writers are more interested in persuading us that men and women in all periods and places have qualities close to our own—similar virtues and similar faults—and that it is more desirable for us to understand and profit from those than to be concerned with such " quaint " words and phrases as " Gadzooks " and " By my halidom! "

II

James Bridie had reached the age of forty when the first performance of a play by him was given in Glasgow in March 1928, two years before *Tobias and the Angel*, his sixth play, was produced. In the years between the time he left school and the time he began as a playwright his life had tended in a quite different direction and he had lived it under another name, his proper one.

Osborne Henry Mavor was born in " a flat in a decent stone-built building in a residential district of Glasgow called Pollokshields "[1] on 3 January 1888. His grandmother's name was Mary Ann Bridie, his grandfather's James Mavor: he drew upon both for his pen-name when playwriting became his chosen life-work. His father, Henry Mavor, had intended to be a doctor, but became, instead, an engineer and inventor. " He was fond of the English language and abhorred slang ", read various English classics aloud to his son, but saddened his wife by

[1] The quotations in this section are from *One Way of Living*.

not sharing her " deep religious feeling ". Bridie wrote:

> I find it hard to describe my mother's appearance. She had a magnificent head and profile—so magnificent that they would have been intimidating if it had not been for the indescribable gentleness of her expression. Her hair was parted in the middle over a huge forehead and big, deep orbits. There was a Roman look about her finely cut nose. She had a strong, square jaw and a wide, compressed mouth. She always looked (and was) a little anxious. When her father died in his early thirties she was the only really effective member of that big family of girls and, from that time till her death, she thought and planned for them and for an ever increasing circle of all mankind.

The family went to church to please Mrs. Mavor, but James Bridie's chief recollection of his early churchgoing was that the long monotonous sermons made it impossible for him to concentrate upon reading the Bible, which he tried to do while the minister was preaching.

For years the boy was tormented by horrible dreams. As a means of counteracting them he invented two methods, though the first of these seems hardly less terrifying than nightmares: " Before I went to sleep, I shut my eyes tight and saw a number of red devils in blue jackets dancing round a cauldron surrounded by leaping flames. . . . It [was] wonderfully effective." The second method was to utter " an invocation to birds, beasts, flowers and Jesus. . . . If I felt uneasiness and strangeness coming over me when I was asleep I had only to repeat that . . . and I woke, quiet and comforted."

Very early he decided to be a doctor, but, he said, only because he was very lazy and noticed that " the Doctor with whose children I used to play owned a brougham ". He thought that as a doctor he would always be able to ride about and not have the trouble of walking. But though he appeared to be mentally as well as physically indolent, he was only about four years old when—fired by Shakespeare, " the only good influence in my early life to which I did not put up a sturdy and mulish resistance "—he began to write " a Drama on the life of King Robert the Bruce. One complete scene survives:

> *Scene: The English Camp. Enter the Earl of Pembroke.*
>
> THE EARL OF PEMBROKE: I wonder what these devils of Scotsmen are up to now.
>
> (*Exit the Earl of Pembroke*)."

After attending infant schools and, for a year, Glasgow High School, he went to Glasgow Academy, where he was much bullied. In the Junior School there he won second prizes and, later, in the Senior School the mathematics master declared " Mavor's got the best head in the class. In fifteen or maybe sixteen years, you'll hear about Mavor. He'll beat ivery one of ye." Though it was some twenty-five or more years before Mavor was " heard about ", and then under another name, this was a declaration which showed prophetic foresight by the master they called " Snubs " and whose Scots accent they made game of.

Soon after Bridie (as it is now more convenient to call him) was fifteen and had already passed the preliminary examination in medicine, he started practical anatomy at the University of Glasgow.

Looking back and recognizing that to others he appeared in early life unattractive both in appearance and in character, he wrote:

> My father did not make me a scholar and a scientist, but he gave me a curious code of honour which I have seldom transgressed, and a faculty for enjoying the manifestations of greatness, goodness and workmanship whenever I meet them. My mother did not make me a good or methodical man, but she taught me tolerance and loyalty. In my first twenty-five years appreciation, tolerance and loyalty kept breaking out in spite of me. I may have been repulsive, but I was not bad.

Even though he made extremely slow progress with his medical studies at the university, his non-academic and apparently time-wasting activities were preparing him for the life-work that was still hidden from him. He developed his knowledge of people by going to a good many parties: " I found these . . . very enjoyable and grew very fond of the people I met at them, though I seldom exchanged two words with them." He observed attentively and stored the knowledge of human behaviour thus acquired.

Also he went frequently to the theatre. Among the plays he saw was *Peter Pan*, by the author who was at that time the most outstanding modern playwright Scotland had produced, but who was afterwards to be overshadowed by the author of *Tobias and the Angel.* Of *Peter Pan* Bridie wrote, thirty years later:

> I have an idea now that I was wrong in admiring it. Boys who never grow up are not agreeable characters in real life. Barrie should have been better grounded in the doctrine of Original Sin than to have invented such a character. He observed truly, but deliberately obscured the cruelty, irresponsibility and lies which were the principal features of his matchless boy.

He nevertheless regarded J. M. Barrie as a genius because he considered him the " only legitimate descendant of the ballad writers ", sharing with them " the knack with which the strange mixed races of the borders used to frighten each other at night ", " their real magic—that drawing aside quickly and as suddenly dropping back of the veil before we have time to see what is beyond ", the sense of mystery which haunts because it is beyond explanation.

Bridie divided his autobiography into chapters each covering five years. Of himself in " The Fourth Five " he said: " I do not know why I dislike Number Four so much. I have shown him [as] a giggling, jeering, lethargic oaf. He wasn't—he was humble and he had the endearing quality of being able to enjoy things it was decent to enjoy." During that period the great stumbling block to progress in his medical studies was Anatomy, in which he failed time after time. On the first occasion the examiner said " I suppose it is no secret to you that you know nothing at all about Anatomy? You'll never be a doctor. Run away and be an artist." It was advice he did not intentionally take, and years were to pass before he became an artist in words; but he was already learning that the true value of an artist is that " he teaches us to see. He teaches us to look at things we have never noticed. The play of light on a bird's wing. The pattern of interlacing branches." The literary artist does still more than this: he teaches us to see in human beings many things we have not noticed before; and by seeing, by sharpening our vision, we reach understanding.

Meanwhile Bridie made up for his lack of distinction as a student by seeking distinction as a buffoon:

> I wore a battered bowler hat with a hole in the crown. I wore a red neck-tie, a jacket the colour of tomato soup, a waistcoat from another suit and a pair of magenta trousers striped with mauve which had belonged to my grandfather. My socks were blue with horizontal black stripes, and my shoes were brown brogues. As if this were not enough I also wore a monocle.

He wrote verse and prose (including dramatic criticism) for the Glasgow University Magazine and became one of its editors. He also experimented with play-writing and had several pieces " performed to loud applause at various undergraduate functions ".

At last, in 1913 when he was twenty-five, he qualified and became a doctor on the staff of the Royal Infirmary in Glasgow, but before he could get far in his career the First World War took him into the R.A.M.C. After a period of service in France and Belgium he spent the rest of the war period in India, Mesopotamia, Persia, Transcaucasia and Constantinople and told about his experiences in those places in his first book, *Some Talk of Alexander* (1926), the title being a phrase from a well-known patriotic song " The British Grenadiers ", though it was also an allusion to Alexander the Great whose conquests were in that region. The importance of this period was that it made Bridie familiar with the territories in which *Tobias and the Angel* is set.

On returning to Scotland in 1919 Bridie bought a medical practice in Glasgow. In dealing with patients he " learnt to appreciate courage and self-sacrifice in everday life " and to distrust and avoid sentimentality. But he was not happy in his profession and wrote a good deal, hoping to make money, though from that source he earned only about £7 in three years. " One thing I did not write for money. It was a three-act play and I wrote it to see whether I could write a three-act play." A theatre director to whom he sent it said that it was very clever, but that no manager would risk money on it. " I accepted his verdict, put the play in a drawer and forgot all about it."

He married in 1923, when his bank balance was only £13 and a few shillings. Though he did not give up medical work for several years after that, he was soon to be drawn into the company of people connected with the theatre, and at this point it is necessary to say something about an important Scottish enterprise in which Bridie was to have a leading part.

III

From the Middle Ages onward Scotland has had many fine poets, but few distinguished playwrights. This may be due more to religious causes than to any natural lack of dramatic genius. In the sixteenth century Sir David Lyndsay wrote a very long play called *A Pleasant Satire of the Three Estates in Commendation of Virtue and Vituperation of Vice*. It is extremely complicated in plot and in manner, being both sacred and profane, sternly allegorical and wildly farcical. Numerous characters from bury the dead, I was with thee likewise. . . . And now God hath sent me to heal thee and Sara thy daughter in law. . . . Now therefore give God thanks: for I go up to him that sent me; but write all things which are done in a book." Tobit and Tobias " fell upon their faces: for they feared "; " And when they arose, they saw him no more ".

Tobit was fifty-eight when he lost his sight and it was restored to him after eight years. He lived to be " an hundred and eight and fifty years ", and after he and Anna died Tobias and his wife and six sons went to Ecbatane, where he lived until he was " an hundred and seven and twenty years old ".

The foregoing summary of the Book of Tobit enables a comparison to be made with *Tobias and the Angel*, whereby we learn something of the process of literary creation—the way in which the essentials of an antique story and even snatches of its phraseology can be retained when it is presented in a new form, and the degree in which departures may be made from the original in order to give fresh power and new beauty to an old and imperishable tale.

We see that Bridie kept close to the main outlines, reduced the religious detail, greatly developed the characterization, introduced humour, and used modern colloquial speech and references. When we read the Book of Tobit we are conscious throughout that, although the story is fascinating, the people appear to be unlike ourselves; that their ways are not our ways, and that the duties which earn them divine reward are expressed in terms so general as to seem vague. When Raphael at length tells Tobit and Tobias why he had been sent to their aid, he instructs them to bless, praise and magnify God, to reveal his works, to devote themselves to prayer, fasting, alms, and righteousness, and to bury the dead. We do ourselves, of course, accept as a duty the burial (or cremation) of the dead, but we do not regard it as first and foremost a sacred ritual which, when performed, earns divine reward, and if neglected brings divine punishment. (We must not, however, overlook the possibility that the ritual significance of burial may have developed originally from hygienic necessity, since exposed bodies could cause disease and disease could be regarded as a divine affliction indicating God's anger.) The other duties enumerated by Raphael are all praiseworthy, but, for example, though it behoves all of us to be righteous, we need (though perhaps only because of spiritual ignorance and blindness) to be told something about the nature of righteousness and how in daily life we may achieve it.

Since these are large matters that could not be examined in the brief compass of a stage play, Bridie devotes attention to more homely things and lets us see something of the small follies which make men and women less good than they might be and make life less pleasant than it could be: Tobias's conceit and self-praise when he claims credit for achievements which were not his but were due to supernatural aid—

> Did Azarias run the risk of being strangled by Asmoday? No! Did Azarias terrify the bandit who attacked us on the road near Asshur? No! Did Azarias fight the devil-fish! No! Who did? I did.

Sara's light-headed flirtation with an Archangel as more romantic than devotion to an " ordinary " husband, so that Raphael is compelled to rebuke her soundly—

> Sara, you have the mind of a child and the instincts of an animal. You have a smooth, weak, meaningless face. When your face moves prettily it is play-acting. When it is moved by emotion it is ugly beyond speaking about. When you take off your shoes you walk like a duck. Your whole body is a compound of absurdities and irrelevances. Your only admirable feature is the magnificent impudence that impels you to make sheep's eyes at an Archangel six thousand years your senior.

In that passage, as elsewhere in Raphael's part in the play, plain truth and humour are combined. So, too, Anna is absurd when she resorts to that threadbare female fiction, "woman's instinct", to justify her weeping and moaning when she supposes that Tobias is dead. Self-conceit; flirtatiousness; sentimentality: we think of these as minor faults, but they add up to major sources of friction in daily life.

Although it is improbable that Bridie wrote *Tobias and the Angel* as a morality play intended to teach us how to behave, he was certainly not indifferent to mankind's need of the Good Life. The Good Life, however, has in actual practice to be extracted from faulty human material, and so it is in *Tobias*. The faults of Tobias, Sara, and Anna are not fatal; the good in all three outweighs what in them is less good.

Bridie's great achievement in *Tobias and the Angel* is that he humanized the original story without lessening its dignity. The characters are lovable, and although Raphael is a miracle-worker he, too, attracts affection rather than awe. The play is also thoroughly well-made—efficiently jointed and balanced, with a beginning, a middle, and an end; it goes far towards proving that if Bridie had not so often attempted to dramatize subjects which overburdened his creative powers, he could not have been chided for so often ending unsatisfactorily what he so often excitingly began. *Tobias* ends in the beauty of utter simplicity. The Archangel has gone and the last words are Tobit's:

We have been visited.

TOBIAS AND THE ANGEL

The Play was first performed by MR. ANMER HALL'S *Company at the Festival Theatre, Cambridge, on November 20th,* 1930, *with the following Cast:*

TOBIT	Waldo Wright.
TOBIAS	Frederick Piper.
ANNA	Gillian Scaife.
RAPHAEL	Tyrone Guthrie.
BANDIT	Philip Hatfield.
SARA	Marion Anderson.
SHERAH	Barbara Nixon.
AZORAH	Joan White.
TAMKAH	Flora Robson.
KISH	Rupert Doone.
NUBIAN SLAVE	Robert Eddison.
RAGUEL	Roy Malcolm.
ASMODAY	Pascoe Thornton.
GIRLS	Isobel Scaife. Maisie Lambeth. Norah Brown.

The play was produced by Evan John. Miss Robson sang and Mr. Doone danced to a setting of "The Jackal Song" by Mr. Bernard Ord. The characters of Tamkah and Kish were introduced through exigencies of casting.

PERSONS IN THE PLAY

TOBIT	A poor Jew.
TOBIAS	His son.
THE ARCHANGEL RAPHAEL.	
ANNA	Tobit's wife.
SHERAH	A Singing-girl.
SARA	Raguel's daughter.
AZORAH	A Dancer.
RAGUEL.	A rich Jew.
ASMODAY	A Demon.

A Bandit.
An Ethiopian Slave.
Girls in attendance on SARA.

The SCENE is laid in Mesopotamia and in Northern Persia. The TIME is before the reign of Ahasuerus.

Act I, Scene 1: TOBIT's hovel in Nineveh. Scene 2: On the banks of the Tigris, a day's march from Nineveh.

Act II, Scene 1: RAGUEL's house in Hamadan. Scene 2: The same.

Act III, Scene 1: A khan near Kifri. Scene 2: A lane in Nineveh, outside TOBIT's hovel.

TOBIAS AND THE ANGEL

ACT I

SCENE I

TOBIT'S *house in a Nineveh slum. The walls are of baked mud. The room is lit by a largish door on the right. A broad beam of sunlight passes through it. There are the ashes of a fire in one corner, and the chimney is a hole in the roof. The furniture consists of two low broad benches, covered with ragged rugs. The seven-branched candlestick is on one bench;* TOBIT, *blind and ragged, on the other. He is a handsome little fat man of sixty-six. He is bald, and his little spade beard has been red, but is now almost white. He gets up to look for his stick. He almost knocks over the candlestick, but saves it just in time.*

TOBIT. Tut, tut. Clumsy old fellow. Tottering about like a sturdied sheep. My stick. My stick. Now where did I leave my stick? Dear, dear, I'll be forgetting my prayers next. Let me think. Let me think. I was thinking about my grandmother and I sat down there. Or was it there? I must get my bearings. This bit of the floor is warm. Yes. That's the door. The sun is streaming in. It can't be long before sunset. Now the stick must be over there in the nor'-east corner. Stick, stick, where are you? It isn't very loyal of you to forget me like this. It isn't like you at all to leave your poor old blind centipede without his antenna. It isn't here. How awkward. And I wanted to go for a walk. The Governor's garden is nice in the cool of the evening. The almond blossoms are falling and I can't find my stick. What a misfortune. (*A Dog barks.*) That's Toby at last. I can hear him snuffling and the patter of his little feet. Tobias can't be far off. Tobias! Hurry, Tobias, and help me to find my stick.

[*Enter* TOBIAS *and his dog.* TOBIAS *is a little fat young man with reddish fair hair becoming prematurely bald. The dog is a well-trained mongrel.*

TOBIAS. Well, daddy. Had your walk yet?

TOBIT. No, not yet, sonny. I can't find my stick, somehow. I've been trying to think where I put it, but my wits have gone wool-gathering as usual, and I can't remember.

TOBIAS. Here it is, daddy; you should keep hold of it.

TOBIT. Oh, thank you, thank you. You are a great comfort to me, sonny, and I am a proper old nuisance. I am like an old bat fluttering about the room in the twilight. I nearly knocked down the seven-branched candlestick. What do you think of that? Isn't it lucky we aren't still in our fine house in Leviathan Avenue? I'd have broken the Chaldean vases and tumbled down the marble stairs, and bumped myself all over in the corridors.

TOBIAS. We could have afforded a couple of slaves to lead you about.

TOBIT. I suppose we could. But, do you know, sonny, I never got quite used to a great houseful of slaves. I did hate bothering them. And they said whatever they liked to me. You remember that fellow Rasik, my head valet?

TOBIAS. Don't I just! Mother and I always say that if he had looked after you properly and had chased away the sparrows from your bed in the courtyard, you would never have got cataract, and you would be able to see to-day.

TOBIT. No, no. You mustn't talk like that. You mustn't blame Rasik and the poor little sparrows for an act of God.

TOBIAS. He was a slovenly, careless, big, black bully, anyhow. He bullied you.

TOBIT. Oh, not very much. Not very much. No more than one expects to be bullied by one's servants. (*He laughs.*) But he always used to make my bath either too hot or too cold. I remember one day saying, "Rasik, don't they give you enough to eat in the kitchen?" And he said, "Oh, so-so." And I said, "Are you boiling your unfortunate master because you are hungry? If you are, please give my compliments to cook and tell her I prefer to be served with caper-sauce." Joking with him, you see. And Rasik said, "Apple-sauce and beans more likely." I thought that was going a bit too far. I mean, I like a joke as well as anyone, but he knew quite well what my religious convictions were on the subject of pig, so I said, "Rasik," I said, "I sometimes doubt if you realise where wit stops and impertinence begins." And he said, in quite an impudent voice, "Ho!" he said, "Ho! You are only a Jew after all." *Only*, mind you! And I said, "Rasik, I don't think that is any way to speak to your employer." And Rasik said . . .

TOBIAS. Long before the conversation had reached that point, I think I should have ordered him a dose of bastinado.

TOBIT. I suppose that would have been a sort of a repartee.

TOBIAS. And a very good one.

TOBIT. No, no, sonny. I don't think you realise how painful the bastinado can be. It is worse than bunions, and I have had both.

TOBIAS. I know, daddy. But the fact remains that you were always too good-natured with servants and everyone else. And look where it has brought us.

TOBIT. Well? Isn't it nice? I have no more servants to bother me now. Only you and mamma.

TOBIAS. I know. You always say it makes life easier to be poor; but it is hard on mamma, after being head of a big establishment to go out scrubbing offices all day.

TOBIT. It is perhaps a little humiliating. But humiliation is a splendid tonic. And the work is hard, but it keeps her so fit. I remember she had terrible pains in the abdomen whenever I stayed out a little late at a meeting; and most frightful headaches whenever I asked some unfortunate Jewish brother to dinner. And it was all for want of regular exercise. Doctors were never out of the house. And now she has nothing but housemaid's knee, and she says it isn't very bad. I'm sorry for you though, sonny.

TOBIAS. Oh, I'm all right, really. It's much better fun running errands and holding horses and fishing and knocking about with my dog than spending my days in that snobbish, boring university, and my nights making myself sick at dinner-parties and pretending to be in love with screeching dancing-girls. You have the worst of it yourself.

TOBIT. I'm sorry I can't go to Jerusalem now. I feel it more at this time of the year—round about Pentecost. I always used to go to Jerusalem.

TOBIAS. It doesn't look like a very lively Pentecost for us.

TOBIT. Oh, indeed it may not be so bad. My nephew, Achiacharus, may remember us again this year, the kind fellow.

TOBIAS. Achiacharus! If I were the King's accountant I think I should be ashamed to allow my own uncle to live in a hovel.

TOBIT. Now, now, Tobias. Achiacharus has been very kind. He is a very busy man. I had hoped he might have found a job for you somewhere, sonny, but he is quite right to have no favourites, quite right.

TOBIAS. I wish I had caught a fish to-day.

TOBIT. It is the happier for the fish that you haven't. Your mother may bring something home.

TOBIAS. I should have caught a fish. But there was a crowd of Assyrian loafers fishing from the jetty and I was afraid. You remember last week they beat me and threw me in the river for pushing in among them. And I wasn't pushing hard either.

TOBIT. I am sure you weren't, sonny. It is strange that you are timid. Your mother isn't timid since the Lord took away our money. And I don't seem to be much afraid of anything.

TOBIAS. That is true. You are as brave as a lion. But that is because you belong to a generation that had no nerves. We of the new generation are all much more temperamental and highly strung.

TOBIT. It is true of all new generations. Our father Adam must have been a very tough gentleman indeed, I often think. It is a great misfortune for you, sonny, that you are so timid. I cannot be glad enough that you were born too late to see the burning and ravishing and throat-slitting and pillage that I have seen. . . . Is that your mother?

TOBIAS. I don't hear anything, and Toby hasn't barked.

TOBIT. Go out to the lane and see. Thank God my ears have grown keener since I lost my sight. But it isn't like her step.

TOBIAS. There is no one in the lane, but the little dog's hackles are up and he looks too terrified to bark. Daddy, do you think it's a Djinn?

TOBIT. Very unlikely. Djinns and Afreets don't bother poor folk.

TOBIAS. I wish I thought so.

TOBIT. Are you frightened, sonny?

TOBIAS. Yes, a bit. I don't know why. It's the dog, I think. I never knew him behave in that way before.

TOBIT. Take my hand, sonny. It is steady, isn't it? Why should you be afraid in the daylight when I am not afraid in the dark? (*The dog yelps outside.*) The poor dog is afraid. I'll go and bring him in.

TOBIAS. No. Don't leave me, father. There's someone coming.

[*They wait. The* ARCHANGEL RAPHAEL *appears at the door disguised as a porter. He carries a great basket. Even in his disguise he is very tall and beautiful. He puts down his basket and stands silhouetted against the evening sun.*

RAPHAEL. Peace be on this house.

TOBIT. And remain with you on all your travels. Thank you very much, sir, for your good wishes. Won't you come in?

TOBIAS. He is only a porter, father. It's all right.

RAPHAEL. Thank you. I will come in. I have brought some roast quails, some pomegranates, some wine and some arrack. They are intended to eke out your Pentecostal dinner.

TOBIT. From my nephew Achiacharus, the King's accountant. How kind of him.

RAPHAEL. My master has a great regard for you, sir.

TOBIT. I too have a great regard for him. We are fortunate in such a friend at court. Will you sit down?

RAPHAEL. Who, I? Willingly.

[*He sits on the floor against the wall.*

TOBIT. It must have been hot work carrying all these good things. Will you have a glass of wine?

RAPHAEL. No, I thank you. A little water.

TOBIT. Are you sure?

RAPHAEL. Yes. I am a teetotaller.

TOBIT. As you wish. Far from me be it to force any man to drink against his convictions. It is rare to find any convictions at all these days. Tobias, run out and bring in the water-skin.

[TOBIAS *goes out and returns presently with the chagul.*

He hasn't even forgotten the little dog. How thoughtful of him. Here is a bone for Toby. Tobias, untie Toby and bring him in. We have a treat for him.

TOBIAS (*looking doubtfully at* RAPHAEL). He wouldn't come in, father. It is very strange.

TOBIT. Don't mind my son, Mr. Porter. He is a nervous lad. Strangers upset him. I'll tell you what we shall do. You will stay with us for dinner. Then you won't be a stranger any longer. Give him a cup of water, Tobias. It is so pleasant to find a porter who drinks water.

RAPHAEL. Thank you, Tobias.

TOBIAS. You know my name.

RAPHAEL. Yes. (*He drinks.*) There is nothing wonderful about that. I heard your father calling you Tobias. You have spilled some of the water. You must pull yourself together.

TOBIAS. I don't know what sort of porter you are, but . . .

TOBIT. I am sure he is an excellent porter, or he would not be employed by Achiacharus. Dear me, what strength of character it must require to carry heavy loads all through the hot day and to remain a teetotaller. Well, well. We shall have quite a feast. Very jolly and convivial indeed. Quite like old times. . . . Quite like old times. . . . Quite like . . . Oh, Tobias, miserable old man that I am, I had forgotten.

TOBIAS. Forgotten what, father?

TOBIT. I get stupider every year. Yes, yes. There is enough in the basket for another. The porter, Anna, you, me, Toby. . . . Yes. Tobias, I'm sorry to bother you again, sonny, but I must ask you to go out again.

TOBIAS. What for, daddy?

TOBIT. Surely you know? In my days of prosperity, of which this is one, it is necessary to remember my poor co-religionists who are not so fortunate as I. Go out to the bazaar and bring in the first poor Jew you meet. Unfortunately we have only enough for one. Times have changed, Mr. Porter, but there are still poor Jews.

TOBIAS. But, father, it was all very well when we had enough for ourselves. . . .

TOBIT. Tobias, do as I tell you.

[TOBIAS *goes.*

TOBIT. It was just a sort of old fancy of mine, Porter, when I had money to spend, to ask one or two of my poor brothers to take pot-luck with me. If you are happy yourself, there is no harm in increasing the sum of the happiness, is there? Alas, all I was able to do for many of them was to bury them. These were bad times. The young officers and students used to garrotte the poor fellows. Just thoughtlessness, of course, but a very unpleasant time. I used, some nights, to trot round like an old jackdaw popping poor murdered Hebrews into holes in the ground. I thought it the least I could do. It was a great abuse, this strangling of Hebrews. A great abuse. However, thank God, we have an enlightened King now. Sacherdonas has told my nephew, the King's accountant, in so many words that he doesn't approve of it at all. When he returns from Shusha in a week or so, the King is going to see what can be done about it. He says it is quite barbarous and unworthy of a progressive modern city. And he is perfectly right. Perfectly right. Of course he has the vested interests and the aristocratic die-hards against him, but I have every confidence that before very long the public opinion of Nineveh . . .

Ah! I hear my wife coming into the lane. She has just a little asthma these days when the evening chill begins. This will be a beautiful surprise for her. . . . Anna! Anna, my darling, shut your eyes when you come in by the door. We shall be two old blind bodies for just a few moments. Please do.

ANNA (*outside*). Wait a moment.

TOBIT. Remember to keep your eyes shut till I tell you to open them.

ANNA. Oh, all right.

[ANNA *comes in. She is a sturdy middle-aged woman. She carries a small sack.*

ANNA. What is it, you daft old fool? I've got my eyes shut. . . . Mercy on us, there is a Presence in the room. I'm all of a tremble.

TOBIT. Anna. Don't shake, dear. It's only the porter from Achiacharus. Look, dear. Look what he has sent us.

RAPHAEL. Your servant, ma'am.

ANNA. God be with you, my man. You startled me. What is all this?

TOBIT. From Achiacharus. Wasn't it nice of him to remember us?

ANNA. Hmph. No doubt. I wish his memory were a little less fitful. . . . Well, my man, what are you waiting for?

TOBIT. He is waiting to dine with us, Anna. I have asked him to be our guest, and he has done us that honour.

ANNA (*throwing up her hands*). Oh, well, I suppose he is very welcome. And now perhaps I had better heat up these quails.

[*She lights a little camel-dung fire in the corner and begins to prepare the meal.*

TOBIT. Have you had a hard day, sweetheart?

ANNA. Not particularly, to-day. I was working in the Government offices to-day. It is a pleasant rest to work in the Government offices. It is their reposeful atmosphere that is so soothing. Are you in Government employment, Porter?

RAPHAEL. Yes, in a sense.

ANNA. I thought you looked too fat and healthy to be a casual porter. You are in the accountancy department, of course.

RAPHAEL. No.

ANNA. Where then?

RAPHAEL. The Courts, principally.

ANNA. Oh! I've worked there and I don't recollect your face. Have you been there long?

RAPHAEL. Yes.

ANNA. Well, I've never seen you before. It's curious.

TOBIT. You have to keep looking downwards to your work, Anna dear. You must look up to see a big fellow like the porter here.

ANNA. That may be. Anyway he's the least talkative porter I have ever met.

TOBIT. He hasn't had a chance. What with my monologues and your cross-examinations he hasn't had a chance. Wait till he has had some dinner. Oh, Tobias . . .

[*Enter* TOBIAS, *carrying his dog.*

TOBIAS. Father, I . . .

TOBIT. Did you find a poor Jew ?

TOBIAS. Yes. But he . . . but he had been strangled. Dead. He lay at the edge of the south ditch. His eyes were open.

TOBIT. Dear, dear me. How sad. Some misguided young nobleman has been drinking too much and forgotten himself. Dear me. What a pity. Well, well. Where's my stick ? Ah, yes, yes.

ANNA. Where are you going, father ?

TOBIT. We can't leave the poor fellow out there for the jackals and the pi-dogs and the kites. Come along, Tobias. We must bring him back here and keep him till we can bury him in the morning.

TOBIAS. Father, it's getting dark. He looked awful. I daren't go.

ANNA. And quite right too. Stay where you are, Tobit. A delightful cheery dinner we should have with a corpse in the corner.

TOBIT. Anna, I can't eat a bite while that poor chap is lying out there in the cold.

ANNA. He can't feel the cold now, God rest him.

TOBIT. No. But somehow . . . I can. It's a kind of selfishness, I suppose. And anyhow there's my plain duty. Where did you say he was, sonny ? If you can't come with me I must find him myself.

RAPHAEL. I will go and bury your dead.

TOBIAS. No, no. Come with me and we'll carry him back here. You'd only get into trouble with the town guard if you were found burying a man at sundown.

RAPHAEL. I have had trouble with more formidable beings than the town guard; and they have invariably regretted it more than I have.

TOBIT. But, sir, you are my guest. I cannot allow you to . . .

RAPHAEL. Sit down, Tobit. Sit down, Tobias. I shall be back presently.

[RAPHAEL'S *manner intimidates even* TOBIT. *He lets the Angel go.*

TOBIT. Well, perhaps . . . Dear me. Poor fellow. I hope the porter can find him all right. I hope he doesn't have trouble with the guard. It would be a pity for any of them to be hurt when they are only doing their duty.

ANNA. He seems a violent sort of fellow. And I thought he was very familiar, with his Tobit and his Tobias.

TOBIT. Ah, no. Surely not. He is a fine young fellow. A fine young fellow.

TOBIAS. I think he is a nobleman in disguise making fun of us.

TOBIT. Do you think so? Well, I hope he enjoys the joke. It is pleasant to find a sense of humour in Nineveh. They take themselves so seriously here, and so many of their jokes are in such bad taste. . . . Go after him, Tobias, and see that he finds that poor fellow. Joke or no joke, I should like the poor fellow to get a decent burial.

TOBIAS. I needn't go too near.

TOBIT. No, no. Hurry, hurry.

[TOBIAS *and the dog go out.*

TOBIT. Poor Tobias. He is so frightened, too. It was

nice of him to go. (*A kid bleats at the doorway.*) What's that, Anna?

ANNA. It sounds like a kid bleating.

TOBIT. A kid? What kid?

ANNA. A kid I brought home this evening.

[*She lights a torch in a sconce.*

TOBIT. Anna!

ANNA. What do you mean, Anna?

TOBIT. You must take it back at once. At once, do you hear?

ANNA. Why should I take it back?

TOBIT. Because it is not ours, do you hear? If we can't live without stealing we had better not live at all.

ANNA. Who said it was stolen? It was a present.

TOBIT. Anna, you are too old to receive presents. I still admire you very much, but it is unlikely that anyone else does to the extent that he would give you a valuable present.

ANNA. Ho! You are very flattering. Let me tell you, beautiful, strong, handsome, rich Mister Tobit. . . .

TOBIT. Old friends do not flatter each other. Take back that kid and don't bring grief on our household.

ANNA. Don't bring grief on our household? Oh, listen to that, all you prophets and great angels! There is a joke for you all right! What has there been but grief for eight years? Eh? And why? Because dear old Tobit liked to see his name in every stupid charity subscription list. Because dear old Tobit spent my housekeeping money on making himself snug and comfy inside with self-righteousness; because he liked to hear whining thanks that changed to curses when the beggar got round the corner. Because dear old Tobit brought all the scum and the riffraff of Nineveh into my nice clean dining-room, till no decent people would come to call for fear of carrying away fleas. Because poor old Tobit spoilt his clothes and ruined his reputation creeping out at night to bury good-for-nothing rascals of atheistical Jews who were better dead and should have been eaten. And a fine lot of thanks he got for it too.

And there's that young prig of an Achiacharus with his stuck-up barbarian of a Peloponnesian wife. Round they come about once in two years with their soup and their blankets as if we were paupers. And Tobias getting no education and running about wild with his silly little dog. And what about all those business friends whose debts you cancelled? I suppose they are always dropping in to see if good old Tobit is all right and to have a chat with him over old times? Are they? Are they? Not they. Not one of them. They are laughing at you, do you hear? Laughing at you.

TOBIT. Oh, dear, dear. You must be very miserable, Anna, that all these evil thoughts come out all over you like prickly heat. It's my fault, dear. I made you miserable. I'm a wicked old man.

ANNA. I wish to goodness you were. . . . The kid is all right. Old Jason the Greek gave it to me. He threw it in with my wages. They were a week overdue. He was drunk. . . . I meant it for a surprise for you.

TOBIT. And I thought you were telling lies. Oh, the low, dirty mind I have. God forgive me, I'm of little use in the world.

ANNA. You are not. You are not. It was all the little beast's fault for bleating when it did. You are an old angel. Come, I'll light the other torch and feed the fire. It will cheer me up, and that will make you happy too. Where are those old parchments you were playing with? They'll help to make a blaze.

TOBIT. Here they are, Anna. There's a cold wind now the sun has set.

ANNA. You are sure they are of no importance?

TOBIT. Quite. They are receipted bills, most of them. I liked the feel of them.

ANNA. It is a pity to destroy anything that helps to pass the long dark days for you.

TOBIT. It is a pity to destroy anything at all. But these put foolish thoughts into my head. Burn them, burn them all.

ANNA. Oh, look! Here is the jeweller's bill for my old tiara of ten great topazes. I wonder where the tiara is now? The receipt is yellow with age. Ah, well. . . . There it goes.

TOBIT. Burn them all. Don't read them. It will make your heart ache for the silly, wicked old days . . . when we could help people.

ANNA. Gabael? Gabael? Who was that, Tobit?

TOBIT. Gabael? Oh yes. I remember him. Gabrias's boy. I lent him a matter of ten talents on his note of hand twenty years ago.

ANNA. How many talents?

TOBIT. Ten. I'm almost sure it was ten.

ANNA. Yes, yes. It says ten here. Three thousand shekels.

TOBIT. It seems a lot of money now.

ANNA. It is a lot of money. Has he paid it back?

TOBIT. No. I didn't expect him to. I lent him it because . . .

ANNA. But at what per cent.? Payable when? On what security?

TOBIT. Free of interest, of course. Old Gabrias was very good to me when I was a lad. Besides, I'm not a dirty usurer, whatever else I may be.

ANNA. But there must be interest. He must pay you at the bank rate at least. Is he still alive? Where is he now?

TOBIT. In Media or Persia, I believe. He was starting a scent factory at a place called Rages. He was short of capital and I . . .

ANNA. A scent factory *where?*

TOBIT. Rages, I think the name was.

ANNA. Rages! Oh, Tobit you are a stupid old ass.

TOBIT. I know that, light of my eyes, but I don't follow . . .

ANNA. Did you never hear of Rages spikenard? Of Rages frankincense? Of Gabael's Rages musk? Yes, yes! That's the name.

TOBIT. Yes. Horrible stinks they are. The ladies in the Governor's garden make the air loathsome with them. The other day I felt quite ill. There was a woman . . .

ANNA. Never mind about her. Don't you realise that your friend Gabael . . .

TOBIT. He isn't exactly a friend, dearest. He . . .

ANNA. Don't interrupt. That he must be a millionaire by now?

TOBIT. Well, I am glad if the Lord has prospered him, though I could have wished that he had chosen . . . They say somewhere that money does not stink . . . but I should think . . .

ANNA. Oh, think of your ten talents! Think of what they are now—after twenty years at I don't know what per cent. Listen. We must send Tobias to Rages at once, at once. Ten talents! We could move to a decent house in a decent district! We could have slaves. . . . And no more staircases to scrub!

TOBIT. But Gabael will have forgotten all about it.

ANNA. Well, remind him, man, remind him. Here is his note of hand. Now don't say it would be inconsiderate to remind him, or I shall fall down on the floor and foam at the mouth.

TOBIT. Very well. Whatever you say, dear. After all he will no doubt like to be reminded.

ANNA. Tobias must go. At once. To-morrow before sunrise.

TOBIT. Poor lad! What a terrible journey! It is forty days' march to Rages.

ANNA. He must go, and that is all there is to it. It will do him good. We can't afford to lose any time. Gabael might drop down dead.

TOBIT. Oh, I hope not.

ANNA. I hope not too. You'll tell Tobias he must go?

TOBIT. Yes. I'll tell him. . . . Hush. Here he is.

[TOBIAS, RAPHAEL *and the dog come in. The dog is, by this time, apparently reconciled to the presence of an Angel in the house.*

TOBIT. Well? Well, well? Did you find him? Did you find the poor fellow?

TOBIAS. Yes. This man went straight to the place as if he knew the way already. He had begun to dig when I came up with him. He dug like one of those great engines cutting out the new canal. At every dip of his spade he threw out a little mountain. It was no time before the—before the poor Jew was tucked away safely. Then we said a prayer and came away. You must be very strong.

RAPHAEL. Yes. I am strong.

[*He sits again against the wall and looks at his big hands.*

TOBIT. It was very kind of you. I am very much obliged to you. And now, will you honour us by taking your place at our poor table? I think—(*he sniffs*)—the dinner is ready.

[*The people stand round the bench till* TOBIT *says grace, and then recline on the floor—all except* ANNA, *who serves the meal and eats as she may.* TOBIAS *first carries round the chagul and pours a little water on the hands of* TOBIT *and his guest.*

TOBIT. Oh, Jahveh, bless this food and wine.
And sit among us when we dine.
Protect the poor.
Amen.

Well, Mr. Porter, I cannot see you eat, but I can hear you, and I shall be very vexed if I do not hear you crunching and swallowing heartily. A cup of wine with you, sir. Ah, I forgot. I beg your pardon. You have no objection to others . . . eh?

RAPHAEL. None whatever. On the contrary.

TOBIT. How I wish Achiacharus were here to see the pleasure he is giving. You will tell him, Mr. Porter, how much we enjoyed his kindness?

RAPHAEL. Achiacharus did not send you this dinner.

TOBIT. Eh? Who did, then?

RAPHAEL. I am afraid that must be a secret. Shall we pretend that Jahveh Himself sent it?

TOBIT. Yes. Capital. Let us. It makes it all more exciting and it has the merit of being true. Your health, sir. And your health too, my dear son. You are going on a journey.

TOBIAS. What do you say?

TOBIT. Have you been across the mountains to Media, Mr. Porter?

RAPHAEL. Yes. I have.

TOBIT. They say it is very beautiful in Media, with its great snow-capped hills, coloured like coral, and its fountains and vines, and cool dark green poplar groves and pretty walled gardens.

RAPHAEL. Yes. It is a difficult journey with a pleasant ending.

TOBIT. Ah, yes. Very long and difficult they tell me. There will be dangers to the body, sonny, and dangers to the spirit.

RAPHAEL. Thieves and demons.

TOBIT. So I have heard. So I have heard.

TOBIAS. What is he talking about, mother?

ANNA. Have patience, my lamb. Listen to what he has to say.

TOBIT. I don't know about thieves. You won't have much to steal. But I can guard you against demons. At least I can tell you how to avoid them. . . .

Sonny, when I am dead, bury me . . . and look after your mother always. . . . You were dangerous to her once. . . . Mr. Porter, are you getting all you want? . . . Don't forget the God, sonny, and he will do fairly by you as he does to all good men. If he gives you any money, let the poor have some of it. If you can only give a little, give that and don't be ashamed of it. It is wicked to be ashamed about money, and very foolish too. Even a little charity is a good investment against black days and death and destruction. . . . Aya. I think he'll enjoy the journey, don't you, Mr. Porter? Travel is a grand thing for a young man if he doesn't play the fool with it. It enlarges the soul and enriches the memory. Only you mustn't play the fool. Girls, now, sonny, you'll see them making eyes at you all along the way. They'll tell you with their eyes that you are a fine fellow, but they don't really mean it. They'll waste your time and use up your thoughts till you become like a silly little dog running anxiously about in the sun. Keep your mind busy with proper things sonny, and say to yourself, "I'll marry a Jewish girl, as Noe did, and as Abraham did, and as Isaac and Israel did; and she'll know my ways, and we'll have a son of my own." A son is a great comfort. The best in the world, I think. Are you a married man, sir?

RAPHAEL. No.

TOBIT. You will some day. Young men like you do well in the world. You will do well too, sonny. You are having a great chance now. You will have great gangs of men working for you one day. Pay them well, and pay them promptly. I always used to make a point of that. . . .

I think you will have a happy journey, my son, if you think first before you do anything at all: "Will this make me sick in the stomach to think of afterwards?" Getting drunk, for instance. A very little wine will make you happy if it is going to make you happy at all. Stop, then, when you have had that little, for more will not make you any happier and will be only so much expense. . . . Fill my cup, Anna. Is our friend's cup empty?

RAPHAEL. I am all right, thanks.

TOBIT. I am so sorry. I was forgetting. Where was I? Oh yes—so much more money uselessly spent. And that is great foolishness. I don't want you to take money too seriously, sonny, but it doesn't last for ever, and therefore you should only give it where it will do some good. Money given to gamblers and harlots, for example, only does the poor creatures harm. That's so, isn't it, Mr. Porter?

RAPHAEL. That is so.

TOBIT. Then remember you cannot be expected to know everything, and ask advice where you can get it, and that is everywhere. Advice is quite cheap and often quite useful. And always say your prayers regularly.

TOBIAS. I will, father. But, father, I don't understand. What is this journey?

TOBIT. Didn't I tell you? Dear me, what a doddering old man I am. My thoughts keep running on and I run after them. I'll tell you, sonny.

You will start to-morrow at sun-up. You will take a change of clothes, what money we can get together, and the kid your mother brought to-day. You will hold down the Tigris as far as Asshur. Then you will take the camel track through the foothills to Qasri-shirind. You will ask the way there to the Pai-Tak Pass. A magical great wind will blow on you there and your spirit will be renewed. You will climb through the Pass and you will come to the Rock of Kermanshah, where they will tell you how to get to Ecbatana. In Ecbatana an influential Jew called Raguel, an old friend of mine, will doubtless give you shelter and further directions. He will tell you how to find Gabael, the Jew of Rages. You will give Gabael my kindest regards and ask him if it is convenient for him to return a small matter of talents I advanced him twenty years ago.

Go with God, my son, and steer cautiously the ship of piety in a sea of passions.

TOBIAS. But, father . . . I'll do whatever you tell me, of course. You know best, naturally. . . . But I've never done anything of this sort before . . . and I'm not much of a business man . . . and I've no sense of direction. I'd be simply petrified with fear if night came down in the mountains and I was all alone with the bandits and Djinns and Afreets.

TOBIT. I've been thinking of that. I'll try to arrange company for you. You might join a caravan. Perhaps our guest would take a message to Achiacharus. He may know of some . . .

RAPHAEL (*standing up*). I will go with the young man as his companion.

TOBIT. That is very good of you. Very good of you indeed. You shouldn't lose by it of course. We can't pay very much, but we can scrape together a little. Only . . . well, you see the point is this. . . . You see, Tobias is our only son, and perhaps we have rather spoiled him; but he isn't—I mean, it isn't as if he were an experienced man of the world. He isn't, is he, Anna? He is really younger than his age. And you see, we know so little about you. We haven't asked your name nor your history, and if you don't wish to tell us—well! But you see what I mean? We should have to know what tribe you belong to, and about your family, and so forth.

RAPHAEL. I beg your pardon. I understood that all you wanted was a hired man. If you wish your son to cross the Persian mountains processionally accompanied by my tribe and family, I regret that I have no authority to speak for them.

TOBIT. Now I've offended you. What a miserable old man I am! Please don't be angry. We are naturally nervous about Tobias, and, to put an absurd instance, you might be an Assyrian strangler in disguise, and then where would poor Tobias be? Not that I think you would for a moment, after eating my salt; but stranglers are so impulsive, aren't they?

RAPHAEL. Do I look like an Assyrian strangler?

TOBIT. Not a bit. Not a bit. But then, so few of them do. And in any case, though I like your voice, I don't know what you look like, except that you are tall and dignified and have red hair, like my own.

[*He runs his hand over his own bald head.*

RAPHAEL. Well, then, I am neither an Assyrian nor a strangler. Does that satisfy your worship?

TOBIT. I am very glad to hear it. But it doesn't take us very far in the process of exclusion, does it? There are your opinions, you know. Personally I have met several idolaters and polygamists who are excellent citizens and an example to a great many more orthodox people. But I should hardly like to send my only son on a journey with one. I may be narrow-minded, but I am too old to change my views.

RAPHAEL. You need not change them on my account. My name is Azarias. I am the son of Big Ananias, the Nephthalite.

TOBIT. Now, why on earth didn't you say so before?

RAPHAEL. I hadn't thought of it.

TOBIT. But *I'm* a Nephthalite myself, and I knew your father very well indeed. And his brother Jonathas too. And honest, decent pair of fellows. I met them often on the way to Assembly at Jerusalem. Big Ananias. That accounts for your height. Listen to that, Anna. Isn't it splendid?

ANNA. It is good news that he comes of decent people.

TOBIT. The best stock in Asia. Don't be angry with me, my lad. Of course my son shall go with you.

RAPHAEL. I am glad.

TOBIT. Now about terms. Let me see. Let me see. As you know, I am not a rich man. I am ashamed to offer it to the son of Ananias, but what do you say to a drachma a day and all found and, if the trip is a success, a five per cent. bonus when you return? Eh? What do you think?

RAPHAEL. That will do very well.

TOBIT. No, but think, man, think. That is no way to do business. You must haggle a little for better terms. You must behave for a little as if you hadn't heard, could hardly believe your ears, and then as if the offer were an insult. You must pretend to go away in disgust. This is a business proposition, and business must be done decently and in order.

RAPHAEL. I am like your son. I am not a business man. I will do what you ask for the wages you have proposed.

ANNA. And the Lord knows where we shall raise them.

TOBIT. But this is like stepping on a step that isn't there. I am certain Big Ananias never taught you to do business in such a mooncalf fashion.

RAPHAEL. I can take no more than what you have offered. You may—what is the expression?—take it or leave it.

TOBIT. Well, it is extremely irregular. Irregular in the extreme. But you seem a determined young man. To be quite candid I am very glad you have taken this line. I shall not argue with you. So be it. Strike hands. (*They strike hands.*) So that's settled. Now, you must make a very early start to-morrow. What about going to bed? We must be up bright and early. . . . Oh, the dinner!

TOBIAS. We had almost finished.

TOBIT. But this was to be a feast. There were to be speeches and songs and stories, and I have spent the whole evening yattering and yammering like an old bull-frog. What must you think of us, Azarias?

RAPHAEL. I think you are a most respectable old gentleman. And now it is time my young travelling companion was in his bed.

TOBIT. You are quite right, Azarias. You fill me with confidence. Bye-byes. Bye-byes. We shall first, however, say grace after meat and our evening hymn. Anna, leave those pots alone.

I will extol Jahveh that liveth for ever: blessed be his kingdom.

For he doth scourge and has mercy, he leadeth down to hell and bringeth up again: neither is there any that can avoid his hand.

Confess him before the Gentiles, ye Children of Israel: for he hath scattered us among them.

O Jerusalem, the Holy City, blessed are they which love thee: for they shall rejoice in thy peace.

O blessed are they which have been sorrowful for all thy scourgings: for they shall rejoice for thee when they have seen all thy glory, and shall be glad for ever.

Let my soul bless Jahveh, the great King. . . .

For Jerusalem shall be built up with sapphire and with emerald: and all her streets shall say, Alleluia.

Amen and Amen.

And now, my son, God send you a good journey. Go then with this man, and God, who is in heaven, prosper your journey, and the Angel of God keep you company.

[*He kisses* TOBIAS.

We sleep under the stars, Azarias, against the wall of the hut.

RAPHAEL. Go, then. I shall sit by the fire for a little.

TOBIT. Good-night, then, and God bless you.

ANNA. God bless you, Azarias.

TOBIAS. God bless you, Azarias. The dog is friends with you now.

RAPHAEL. And God bless *you*.

[TOBIT, ANNA *and* TOBIAS *gather their blankets and go out.* RAPHAEL *pulls a bench towards the dying fire and sits on the bench. As he stares into the glow a pale aureole appears behind his head, framing it and throwing his face into shadow. The lights go out slowly till only the aureole and the Angel's profile are seen.*

CURTAIN.

SCENE II

The east bank of the Tigris, almost a day's march from Nineveh. Above the ridge of the bank the sky tapers up from dusty brass, through bronze and olive-green to bright blue. No horizon is seen.

TOBIAS, *tired and hot, is sitting on his pack.* RAPHAEL *is standing with his back to the auditorium looking across the Tigris. He, too, has taken off his pack.*

RAPHAEL. Are you tired?

TOBIAS. Tired! My back and legs are made of aches and pains instead of bones and muscles. My feet are red-hot. My stomach is flopping about my ankles. The only light thing about me is my head.

RAPHAEL. You must be in very inferior training.

TOBIAS. Well, you see, I spend most of this part of the year sleeping in the shade of the Governor's date palms. I am not very much used to walking.

RAPHAEL. I am not used to walking either.

TOBIAS. I should have thought you were. How do you get about? You fly, I suppose?

RAPHAEL. Yes.

TOBIAS. I see. You are going to tell me another story. I like your stories very much, Azarias, but don't you think we could have something to eat?

RAPHAEL. Not yet. You are too hot and tired. It would make you ill. I think a swim would freshen you up. Can you swim?

TOBIAS. It is very nearly the only thing I can do. I would have made a very good trout.

RAPHAEL. Well, take your clothes off and get into the river.

TOBIAS. Now that is what I should call a good idea. Isn't it, Tobykins? Are you hot and dusty too, old dog? Come and have a nice swim with master. I say, you are full of good ideas, Azarias. Are you coming in too?

RAPHAEL. No. Not just now.

TOBIAS. Oh, why not?

RAPHAEL. If you must know, I have a slight abnormality in the region of my shoulder-blades. Nothing much, but I am sensitive on these matters. I always bathe alone.

TOBIAS. You are a funny chap. I have two birthmarks and a crop of pimples, but it doesn't worry me. I don't see why any thingummy on your shoulder-blades should worry you.

RAPHAEL. Will you kindly change the subject?

TOBIAS. What is it? Psoriasis?

RAPHAEL. Get into the water. We have a fair distance to go before nightfall.

TOBIAS. Righto. You *are* a bully, Azarias.

[*He disappears below the ridge, the dog with him.*

TOBIAS (*his head and shoulders appearing over the ridge*). I'll tell what you are like, Azarias. You are like a cock-eyed cannibal my father had for a valet when we were camel-borne gentry. Rasik, his name was. The cheek he used to give the old man. I would have had him bastinadoed. But I think it would have hurt the old man just as much as it hurt Rasik. I honestly do. Isn't he quaint, the old man? Arranging about your salary and so on as if he were still a millionaire living in Leviathan Avenue, instead of. . . . Come along, Tobykins. I'm ready if you are. Let's dive together.

[*A splash. Barks and shrieks of delight.*

TOBIAS' VOICE. Do come in, Azarias. It's gorgeous. Ouch! It's like heaven with the lid off.

RAPHAEL. Don't swim out too far. There are nasty currents in the fairway.

[*He begins to make a fire.*

TOBIAS' VOICE. What say?

RAPHAEL. I said, Don't swim out too far.

TOBIAS' VOICE. Oh, I'm all right. I'm very much all

right. . . . No . . . I'm not. What's this? Azarias, help! The fish, the fish! Oh, Azarias, it's swimming round me. It's looking for a place to bite. It's snapping at me. Oh, Azarias, its teeth! its teeth!

RAPHAEL. Don't be a coward. Catch it by the little bags behind its jaw . . . and hold on!

TOBIAS' VOICE. I can't. I can't. Keep away, you brute.

RAPHAEL. Do as I tell you.

TOBIAS' VOICE. It's all very well. . . . Ough! I've got him. By gum, he is strong!

RAPHAEL. Hold on. Hold on tight.

[*The dog, dripping with water, is projected over the ridge.*

That's right. Give a heave and pitch him on to the bank. Now grip him again.

TOBIAS' VOICE. I've got him. I've hit him with my stick. He's dead. By gum, what a monster.

[*He appears, naked except for a loincloth, dragging a gigantic mud-fish.*

TOBIAS. That's him.

RAPHAEL. That's he, you mean.

TOBIAS. He, then. By gum, he gave me a tough fight. It was a bad day for him when he tried to bite me. I hung on like grim death. I'm slow to take hold, but I never let go. That's the sort of man I am. Look at him. There's been nothing like him since the whale coughed up Jonas. Ho! If Jonas had been half the man I am he would have swallowed the whale. Isn't he beautiful, Azarias?

RAPHAEL. He is as beautiful as you are marvellous. The fire is ready for him. You will gut the fish and cook him and cut him into steaks and dry them in the sun. They will be useful on the journey.

TOBIAS. *I* will cook him? Look here, Azarias, am I the hired man or are you?

RAPHAEL. I am the hired man. I am paid to guide

you, and therefore you will do as I direct. Take your knife and gut the fish.

TOBIAS. Oh, very well.

[*He follows* RAPHAEL'S *instructions.*

RAPHAEL. Here is a cloth. Take first his liver and his gall and wrap them up.

TOBIAS. Why?

RAPHAEL. Because I say so. Put them in your pack.

TOBIAS. But why, Azarias? Please tell me why.

RAPHAEL. One never knows when they may come in handy.

TOBIAS. What is the use of a mud-fish's liver?

RAPHAEL. That is at once a physiological and a philosophical problem, Tobias, and I prefer not to answer it at present. Instead I shall tell you a story while you work.

TOBIAS. Thank you very much indeed.

RAPHAEL. Not at all. . . . Once upon a time there was a king's daughter who had eyes like two full moons, teeth like a flock of Angora goats, and cheeks like a parcel of pomegranates swimming in blood.

TOBIAS. By gum, she must have been a pretty girl.

RAPHAEL. She was a lovely lady. But one day she fell ill and faded like a sick papyrus lily in the drought. She became pale and wan and could not move from her couch for the fluttering of her heart. The king's magicians . . .

TOBIAS. A friend of mine once knew a girl who was taken badly that way. She could hardly . . .

RAPHAEL. The king's magicians did what they could. They cast her horoscope not once but many times. They sacrificed a bat, a scorpion, a bull and an adder. They bled two hundred slaves till they died. They gave her a decoction of herbs picked during the transit of Mercury and administered three times a day, with suitable incantations, before food.

TOBIAS. And it was of no use?

RAPHAEL. I should not go the length of saying that, Tobias, but it didn't help the king's daughter. She grew daily worse and worse. The king was at his wits' end.

TOBIAS. How sad for the poor old gentleman.

RAPHAEL. On the borders of his kingdom there dwelt a woodcutter in a mean hut. His youngest son was called Sarabias. He was a half-wit.

The two brothers of Sarabias, who were called Arphaxad and Shimsham . . .

TOBIAS. I beg your pardon, I did not catch the second brother's name.

RAPHAEL. Shimsham. Arphaxad and Shimsham, the brothers of Sarabias, one day made a feast. They ate for the feast a braxy ram.

TOBIAS. Why a braxy ram?

RAPHAEL. They were glad to get it. As was their custom, they threw the offal to Sarabias, who sat by the door in the sun. At that moment one of the king's trumpeters passed rehearsing the latest news from the palace.

TOBIAS. And what was the latest news?

RAPHAEL. That the king's daughter had had nothing to eat for seven days and seven nights. Sarabias was sorry to hear this, and, taking up the liver of the braxy ram, he made what speed he could to the palace.

[*A Kurdish bandit appears behind* RAPHAEL'S *back. His appearance strikes* TOBIAS *with terror, as well it may. He is armed to the teeth.*

TOBIAS. Oh, *look*, Azarias! Look! Look!

[RAPHAEL *stops his story and looks at his hands. He does not turn round.*

THE BANDIT. *Salaam aleikum.* I perceive you have been indulging in the gentle pastime of angling. A happy sport, by Allah! And perhaps the one a judicious person would choose for his last day on earth. For most unfortunately you have chosen the stretch of river held sacred by my fathers to pollute it with your lines and bait.

So you must die, you two young men. And die, I fear, most horribly. But I am a humane man, and as I see, sir, that you are a foul Jehudi, I can only conclude that, like the rest of your repulsive race, you are dripping with gold, jewels and precious stones. To pass the time pleasantly for a few minutes, I am prepared to bargain with you for what no doubt you consider your not entirely worthless lives. Otherwise my duty will impel me to hang you head downwards over your little fire and cut you slowly to death with little cuts.

TOBIAS. What shall we do? Oh, what shall we do?

RAPHAEL (*sotto voce*). What an abominable taste in rhetoric he has. He is Mirza Khan, a Kurdish thief. Tell him to go to Gehannum.

TOBIAS. But he might not like it. He has a face like a devil.

RAPHAEL. Tell him so. Tell him what you have done this afternoon.

THE BANDIT. How unmannerly to whisper. What lack of breeding. Come now, little one, I had the honour to address myself to you. Will you not answer, before I grow impatient?

RAPHAEL. Answer him. Be a man.

TOBIAS. Do you know what I have been doing this afternoon?

THE BANDIT. I do not. But it will have a certain pathetic interest. What have you been doing this afternoon?

TOBIAS. I went down to that little gutter-ditch and walked about upon it. And the first thing I met was a huge and scaly monster which thought, as you think, you ignorant dog, that I was a little no-account. And it barked and roared and bit at me. So I killed it and tore out its liver, and there it is, wrapped up in a cloth. (*He indicates his enormous pack.*) And what I did to that atrocious, fire-breathing river demon I shall do to you, you hairy-toed polecat, you son of a burnt father, for I am only beginning the carnage I feel I must make before sunset.

THE BANDIT. Who are you, my lord?

TOBIAS. I am Suleiman-ibn-Daoud, and this is one of my Afreets. Now depart in peace and trouble me no further.

THE BANDIT. If my lord pleases, I had no idea . . .

TOBIAS. May your blood turn to dog's blood, you father of sixty dogs! Did you hear me tell you to go in peace? Your liver is too white to put beside that of a river dragon, for it is the colour of the dark flames of hell. You are safe from me, pitiful and hideous ape. Only take your ugliness from my pure sight before I repent my mercy.

THE BANDIT. Allah, have pity on a poor ill-used man. Allah protect you, my lord.

[*He withdraws rapidly.*

TOBIAS. Oh, Azarias, will it be all like this? Will it be all like this, our journey?

RAPHAEL. How can I tell?

TOBIAS. But we have scarcely started, and I have not only been dog-weary and footsore, but twice in deadly peril of my life.

RAPHAEL. All life is perilous. Go ahead and cook the fish.

TOBIAS. I couldn't possibly eat a bite.

RAPHAEL. Very well then, give it to me and I will put it in my pack. It is cooler now. We must be going.

TOBIAS. But this isn't the least what I pictured a journey.

RAPHAEL. Nothing is the least as we picture it.

TOBIAS. I shall have a nervous breakdown long before we reach Media. I feel quite ill already.

RAPHAEL. Nonsense. You did very well. I am quite proud of my little master.

TOBIAS. Are you really? I certainly seemed to be able to speak up to that bandit once I got started. I told him off properly, I think. The words seemed to come, somehow. I heard them at the jetty, but I hoped I had forgotten them. And I did very well with the fish too, didn't I ?

RAPHAEL. Yes. But there was no need to lie to the bandit.

TOBIAS. I didn't lie to him.

RAPHAEL. You did. Your story of the fish I forgive you. Everybody exaggerates about fish. But you said you were Solomon. That is very far from being true.

TOBIAS. I didn't know what I was saying. I was excited. I wish I weren't such a coward. I'm afraid of everything, really. I'm even afraid of women.

RAPHAEL. Are you now ?

TOBIAS. Indeed I am.

RAPHAEL. Don't you like them ?

TOBIAS. Very much, but they terrify me.

RAPHAEL. I think then there is at least one more terrifying adventure in store for you. Let us go.

TOBIAS. What do you mean ?

RAPHAEL (*laughing*). Nothing, nothing.

TOBIAS. I was right in one thing I said to the bandit.

RAPHAEL. What was that ?

TOBIAS. I said you were an old Afreet. So you are.

RAPHAEL. There are no such things as Afreets. Come along.

[*They trudge out, the dog following.*

CURTAIN.

END OF ACT ONE.

ACT II

SCENE I

A walled garden attached to RAGUEL'S *house in Ecbatana, or, as we call it now, Hamadan. To the left there is a house wall with a small arched doorway reached by steps; to the left, a little grove. To the back there is a very high wall against which there is a little throne shaded with arbutus blossoms. A water-lily tank is in the middle of the stage. The time is about four o'clock in the afternoon.* SARA *is half sitting, half reclining on her little throne.* SHERAH *is plucking idly at a zither. Four or five female attendants are lying about anyhow down stage.* AZORAH *is standing R., fidgeting and trying an occasional dance step.*

SHERAH. Would you like me to sing to you, my lady?

SARA. Not particularly, but it would be better than making these abominable little noises with your zither.

SHERAH. My lady is very kind.

SARA. You know very well my lady is nothing of the sort. Stop fidgeting, Azorah. Oh, sing, sing, sing!

SHERAH. What shall I sing, my lady?

SARA. Anything. Sing "The Jackal." It may not be pretty but it's true and it's long, and it suits your voice such as it is.

[SHERAH *sings "The Song of the Jackal."* AZORAH *dances a sort of refrain after each stanza.*

The Song of the Jackal

SHERAH.

1. A thousand leagues of scrub-studded sand:
   Greeny-purple under the moon,
 Like the bed of the Sea when the Sea is all dried up:
   Like the cold deserts at the back of the moon.
 A thousand thousand years before I was born:
   I was a lone Lady Jackal singing to the moon.

[AZORAH *dances.*

2. All through the night I sang to the moon:
Like a great round Prince throwing silver to me,
Throwing down shimmering silver for my song:
In reward for my song and in love for me.
Till a tall soldier rode by in the night on his white horse:
And with his little twisted bow he shot me.

[AZORAH *dances.*

3. I was a kitten in the temple at Thebes:
The old Priest knitted socks with a thread of gold.
I played with the ball of golden thread as it rolled on the floor:
The people brought me milk made pink with musky wine in vessels of gold,
And praised my green eyes and brindled fur and my pretty ways;
But a dog came into the temple at night and killed me on a terrace of ivory and gold.

[AZORAH *dances.*

4. I was a jaguar in a dark green forest:
I crouched on the branches dappled with shade.
My silken skin rippled over my smooth, tough muscles;
My cruel hot eyes burned holes in the shade.
I leaped on the little tethered goat like a thunderbolt:
And the Nigger's sharp spear laid me dead in the shade.

[AZORAH *dances.*

5. I am the wife of a Cadi in Samarcand:
He sits and smokes from a feeding-bottle all day long.
He has crimson lips and a great beard like black velvet:
And he never looks at me all day long.
I look through my small latticed window, I tear the palm-leaf matting:
I blow bits of fluff from the carpet into the hot air all day long.

[AZORAH *dances.*

6. But at night when the moon is shining, when the moon is full:
I roam like a jaguar, I sport like a kitten, I howl like a jackal all night long.

[AZORAH *dances.*

[*The Singer and the Dancer make obeisance and retire sulkily down stage. Half-way through the song,* TOBIAS' *head appears above the garden wall. He goggles on the scene. No one notices him.*

SARA. How fat you Persian girls become! You lie about and eat sugared gelatine all day. It is a perfect disgrace. Azorah is the only one of you who keeps anything like a figure, and she is a Circassian and not a Persian at all. Azorah, why don't you teach them to dance?

AZORAH. It is wasted labour to teach cows to dance.

SHERAH. You nasty, ill-tongued daughter of misfortune! What do you mean?

SARA. Hold your tongue Sherah. Your voice is bad enough when you sing. When you quarrel it is hellish. Come, I'll give you some exercise myself. Let us play at ball.

OMNES. Oh, no! It is too hot. We are too tired. Have a heart, my lady.

SARA. If you don't do as I tell you I'll send for my father and have you all whipped. Where did you put the ball, Azorah?

AZORAH. Here it is, Mistress.

SARA. Come along then.

[*They take off their outer garments. Decency should be preserved, but it is essential that enough of* SARA *should be visible to prove to* TOBIAS *that she is a well-built, graceful, athletic young female. They range themselves in a semi-circle and pass the ball from hand to hand. The first girl to drop it goes into the middle and tries, uttering shrill squeals, to intercept the ball as it flies round and back and forwards.* SARA *is easily the best player, with* AZORAH *a good second.* AZORAH *misses the ball and goes into the middle with a bad grace. The ball comes to* SARA, *and* AZORAH *grabs it before she has time to throw.*

SARA. You can't do that, Azorah. Play the game, please.

AZORAH. That is the game. To get the ball. I've got it. You go into the ring.

SARA. I'll do nothing of the sort. You must wait till the ball is in the air. You can't grab it that way, like a bird of prey.

AZORAH. What nonsense! I've played ball in the Caucasus with professionals and I know what I'm talking about.

SARA. You can't try your village tricks here. Give me that ball.

AZORAH. Certainly not. I won it quite fairly. If you don't know the game you should learn it before making an exhibition of yourself.

SARA. Azorah, you forget yourself!

AZORAH. I come of a better family than you, you vulgar Jewess. Yes, Madame Asmoday!

[*The maids give a cry of horror.*

SARA. What was that you said?

AZORAH. I said "Madame Asmoday!" You're the wife of a demon! Everyone knows it!

[SARA *catches her by the throat.*

AZORAH. That's right. Strangle me! Strangle me! You've strangled seven husbands, strangle me too, Sara the Strangler! Madame Asmoday! Demon's wife! Ha!

[SARA, *furious, throws* AZORAH *down, takes a whip from the garden seat and begins to beat her.*

AZORAH. Witch! Harlot! You've had seven husbands, all of them buried! Where are your sons, witch? Strangle *yourself*, barren witch! Madame Asmoday!

[SARA *drops her whip.*

SARA (*quietly*). Go into the house. All of you.

[*The maids steal away;* AZORAH, *sobbing, between two of them.* SARA *sits on her throne staring in front of her.*

RAPHAEL (*unseen*). Speak to her.

TOBIAS. Young lady!

SARA (*snatching up a veil*). Who are you? What are you doing there?

TOBIAS. I am standing on a gentleman's head.

SARA. Go away at once. I'll call the guard and have you strangled and thrown to the foxes.

TOBIAS. No, no. Please don't do that. It would only make you more unhappy still.

SARA. How dare you stand there? This is a private garden! How long have you been there?

TOBIAS. For about twenty minutes I think.

SARA. Oh! How dreadful!

TOBIAS. Azarias! I say, Azarias! Don't go away! I'll fall. Help me down. I don't want to stay here. There's a young lady here in a frightful rage. Azarias!

[RAPHAEL *has obviously left him and he is hanging on to the top of the wall.* RAGUEL *appears in the doorway of the house. He is a tall, thin fussy man, very richly dressed. He is followed by an Æthiopian archer.*

RAGUEL. What is the meaning of this? Who is this young man, Sara? Sam, put an arrow into him. No, stop. Wait a minute.

TOBIAS. Yes, yes. Wait a minute. Please do. I can explain. Azarias!

RAGUEL. He has a gang with him.

TOBIAS. No, I haven't. Even my hired man has run away. Dear me, what a dreadful position. Don't let your Æthiopian shoot at me, sir. I'm all right really.

RAGUEL. Sara, is he a friend of yours?

SARA. Most certainly not. He is a complete stranger to me. He is a spy.

RAGUEL. Sara, you are . . . Did he see you improperly dressed?

TOBIAS. No, no. I assure you. Nothing of the sort.

SARA. Yes. He did. I was playing ball with the girls. I have never been so insulted in my life.

RAGUEL. But I mean, it was not entirely . . .

SARA. No, no. Of course not. But it was bad enough.

RAGUEL. Do you think Sam had better shoot him?

SARA. No. We've had enough of that sort of thing. Give him a beating and let him go.

RAGUEL. Sam, go round to the front gate and tell the guard to see that he doesn't escape. Then come back here at once. Bring your bamboo stick.

[*The negro goes out through the door.*

Well, sir?

TOBIAS. Look here, don't give me a beating. I had no idea the young ladies would be here. Azarias told me to look over the wall. He said this might be Raguel's place.

RAGUEL. He did, did he? Well, this is Raguel's place.

TOBIAS. Oh, is it? Are you Raguel?

RAGUEL. I am. Who sent you here?

TOBIAS. My father.

RAGUEL. Who is your father?

TOBIAS. Tobit.

SARA. What a funny name!

RAGUEL. Not old Tobit of Nineveh?

TOBIAS. Yes, yes. He's my father. Anna's my mother. Achiacharus, the King's accountant, is my cousin. My name is Tobias.

RAGUEL. Bless my soul! Tobit! Well, well, well. Sam, Sam, come here. Sam! Bring a ladder! Sara, go in, my dear, and put something on. This is Tobit's boy from Nineveh. And how is my dear old friend?

TOBIAS. He is very well, thank you.

RAGUEL. Let's see. He married . . .?

TOBIAS. Anna.

RAGUEL. Of course, of course. You are the son of a good, honest man. Dear old Tobit. Ah, here's the ladder. Come down, come down.

[*The negro brings a ladder and sets it against the wall.* TOBIAS *comes down.*

An active man, Tobit. Never at rest, never at rest.

TOBIAS. He is not so lively, sir, as he used to be.

RAGUEL. Why not?

TOBIAS. He has lost his eyesight.

RAGUEL. Ah, dear me. What a pity! What a pity! It is a great affliction. Poor old Tobit. Take that ladder away, Sam.

[*Negro goes out.*

But he keeps his spirits?

TOBIAS. Wonderfully, wonderfully.

RAGUEL. Darkness is a great plague. Not to see the sunshine. Well, well.

TOBIAS. I have a relative of yours as a travelling companion.

RAGUEL. Have you now? Have you?

TOBIAS. Yes. And he has played me a nice trick. It might have cost me my life. Your Æthiopian might have shot me, and I might have fallen, and lots of things might have happened.

RAGUEL. That is true. I must apologise for my relative. I think his joke was in exceedingly bad taste.

TOBIAS. Oh, he is a pleasant fellow enough, and all's well that ends well. He is a poor relative of yours. In fact he is a distant connection of my own.

RAGUEL. What is his name?

TOBIAS. Azarias.

RAGUEL. Azarias? I don't recall the name. However, he will turn up presently. I expect I shall recognise him. Tobias, this is my daughter Sara. The son of my old friend Tobit, my dear. His arrival at our house was a little unconventional—I shall speak to our relative severely about it—but he is none the less welcome.

TOBIAS. How do you do. I hope I didn't frighten you.

SARA. No, no. I didn't understand. You are very welcome.

TOBIAS. Sir, I have a little dog outside. He will be wondering what has become of me, and for some reason or other he is never quite comfortable with Azarias. Would it be too much to ask you to send your man round for him?

RAGUEL. Not at all. He may find your waggish friend. We shall probably have a good laugh over the whole business to-night. Now you must be hungry, and tired. Sit down, sit down. I'll bring you a small collation myself. It will sharpen your appetite for the evening meal. And my slaves will collect your camels and baggage.

TOBIAS. Alas! A Kurdish bandit stole my camels and I have no baggage except that which my little dog is guarding faithfully outside your garden wall.

RAGUEL. Dear, dear, what a chapter of misfortunes. What a lawless country. Sara, do you entertain Tobias while I see to all this. I'll send Sherah out with a thicker wrap for you. It begins to get chilly here in the late afternoons. Sherah.

[*He goes out.*

SARA. Did you have a pleasant journey?

TOBIAS. Oh, yes, thank you.

SARA. They tell me that Nineveh is very beautiful. We have a song about the Bonnie, Bonnie Banks of the Tigris.

TOBIAS. No. It is not exactly beautiful. It is very formal and flat with its canals and windmills. And we have some dreadful slums.

SARA. How horrid! Are you interested in social welfare?

TOBIAS. No. Not much. My father is. He does quite a lot.

SARA. The gayer side of Nineveh probably appeals to you, doesn't it? It is a gay city, isn't it?

TOBIAS. No. I hardly think so. Rather stiff and standoffish and—well—strict. For instance—— Oh, well.

SARA. Well, what?

TOBIAS. I think it's all nonsense myself; but a—well, an incident like this would be quite impossible in Nineveh.

SARA. Oh, it would be here too, only father and I are very broad-minded. All our neighbours are frightfully provincial, but I think we Jews should show an example in cosmopolitanism, don't you?

TOBIAS. We are not allowed to show our faces, let alone an example, in Nineveh.

SARA. Oh, but that is absurd! You have just told us you have a relative at court!

TOBIAS. That is only because he is good at mathematics. Things aren't so bad as they used to be, I must say, and the king is beginning to appreciate what is left of us. But still——

SARA. I think you are trying to depress me. Or perhaps you are making fun of me. You think I am just a poor Highland girl, with no civilisation and no manners.

TOBIAS. No, Sara. Honestly I don't.

SARA. Then you despise me because you saw my arms and legs, and no young man has any right to see a person's arms and legs.

TOBIAS. Sara, I never saw anything more beautiful in my life—except perhaps that big rose-coloured hill at Kermanshah in the twilight, with the misty, peacock river running round it.

SARA. How tactful of you to change the subject.

TOBIAS. I won't change the subject if you don't wish me to. It is a charming subject and I could meditate on it all afternoon.

SARA. You do despise me! You do! Or you wouldn't talk to me as if I were a dancing-girl. . . . Oh!

TOBIAS. What's the matter?

[RAPHAEL *appears in the grove, unseen by the two.*

SARA. Did you—did you hear what that screeching guinea-fowl said to me in the garden?

TOBIAS. Yes, I heard.

SARA. All of it?

TOBIAS. All of it.

SARA. I must go to my father. I must go in.

TOBIAS. Don't go in. What do I care what she said? Have I never heard a bad-tempered dancing-girl telling lies before?

SARA. You believe they were lies?

TOBIAS. In so far as I could make head or tail of them, I believe they were lies.

SARA. Suppose they weren't? Suppose I had had seven husbands and they had all died on their wedding night?

TOBIAS. I should think, in fear and trembling. . . . I should hope that I too might die such a death, unworthy as I am.

SARA. Don't joke about it.

TOBIAS. Before Abram, Isaac and Israel, I am not joking.

SARA. Tobias, are you a man or a god.

TOBIAS. Do I look like a god? Why do you ask?

SARA. Because there is a god in the garden.

TOBIAS. There is a God everywhere.

SARA. Not that sort of God. Oh, I know, I know, I know. It is terrible to feel the presence of a god.

TOBIAS. Now she's going to faint. What an extraordinary girl!

[*He runs to the tank to get water. He sees* RAPHAEL.

Hello! Azarias! How did you get here? Wait a moment. The young lady has fainted.

[*He throws water on* SARA'S *face.*

That's better, O, my celestial ibis! Full moon

crowned with a myriad stars. O jacinth monument on an ivory plinth, are you feeling better?

SARA. Much better, thank you. Ah! . . . Who is that?

TOBIAS. Oh, that? That's Azarias. He is a cousin of yours.

SARA. I'm afraid of him.

RAPHAEL. Don't be afraid of me, young girl.

TOBIAS. I should think not. You and he are going to be great friends.

[*Enter* SHERAH *with a heavy cloak.*

SHERAH. Lady, your father says you must put this on because it is cold.

SARA. It is not cold.

SHERAH. Well, your father says it is.

SARA. It isn't. Do you think it is?

SHERAH. What does it matter what a slave thinks?

SARA. Take the thing away and don't irritate me.

[*She looks at* TOBIAS *and the Angel. Pauses. Smiles a radiant smile.*

SARA. Very well. If he thinks it is cold it must be cold. Thank you, Sherah. Now we shall go in, if these gentlemen will excuse us.

[*She goes,* SHERAH *following.*

RAPHAEL. Well?

TOBIAS. Oh, Azarias. She is much more beautiful than all the beautiful girls you were telling me about on the journey. When she played at ball she was like a white camel colt leaping in the pastures. My knee-caps turned to jelly and my lungs well-nigh burst in my throat. Her little feet are like two fluttering doves. She runs like an ostrich. She is as brave as a troop of cavalry with dragons' wings and heads like tigers. She has the heart of a rhinoceros and the gentility of a new-born lamb.

RAPHAEL. You have become quite the poet.

TOBIAS. I'm inspired. I'm inspired. An Angel of

the Lord has visited me. I'll write a song for her and you will set it to music. It will be ten thousand times better than that nasty jackal song the stout girl sang. . . . I say, look here, what did you mean by running away and leaving me like that?

RAPHAEL. You were using my head for a dancing floor on which you were performing the horrid dances of Æthiopia. It was time you had a lesson.

TOBIAS. But I might have been shot and flung to the foxes.

RAPHAEL. You would have given them indigestion. You are a tiresome little fellow, Tobias, and I have a good mind to leave you altogether.

TOBIAS. That would be a fine thing with only two-thirds of our journey done. You promised to take me to Rages.

RAPHAEL. You have remembered that, have you?

TOBIAS. Of course. Don't be a pig, Azarias. Azarias, do you think—do you think if I went to Rages and got the ten talents from Gabael and bought a camel or two and half a dozen slaves—do you think her father would allow me to pay my addresses to her? I want her, Azarias. I will have no one else for my wife. She is like a sandstorm beating through a mirage. Her voice is like the massed bands in the Governor's garden on the ninth day of the feast of Baal. Her . . .

RAPHAEL. And therefore you propose to go to Rages and leave her to the first tramp who looks over the wall.

TOBIAS. But oh, Azarias! Look at me! I don't look even a gentleman, let alone a merchant prince. And they are such refined and wealthy people.

RAPHAEL. We shall see about that.

TOBIAS. Mind you, I think she likes me.

RAPHAEL. It is possible that she does. The fancies of a woman are bound by no law.

TOBIAS. All that about the seven husbands? What do you think of it, eh?

RAPHAEL. Here comes her father. You had better ask him.

TOBIAS. Oh, I couldn't.

RAPHAEL. Ha! Killer of the great fish! Ho! Conqueror of Mirza Khan! You are afraid.

TOBIAS. Of course I'm afraid.

RAPHAEL. Then do as I tell you.

[*Enter* RAGUEL *with girls carrying a basin, a ewer, a bottle of wine and some fruit in a great dish.* AZORAH *and* SHERAH *prepare* TOBIAS *for his meal. While they are washing his hands and feet he talks to* RAGUEL.

TOBIAS. Raguel, this is very handsome of you.

RAGUEL. It is the least I could do for your father's son. Ah! Is this your friend?

RAPHAEL. Your servant, sir.

TOBIAS. Yes. This is Azarias.

RAPHAEL. The son of Ananias.

RAGUEL. Indeed? Ah, yes. I didn't know he had a son. However, I am glad to see you. Any friend of Tobias is welcome here. Do you serve your master, or would you prefer to go to the servants' hall. You must be hungry.

RAPHAEL. I shall go to the servants' hall. I am a servant.

TOBIAS. Oh, I say, Azarias . . .

RAPHAEL. I shall go. Remember what I told you.

[*He goes.*

RAGUEL. An extraordinary fellow. I suppose he's faithful enough. But I do feel these people who have come down in the world are a little apt to be familiar, don't you think? Good-looking fellow, though.

TOBIAS. Raguel, it's about Sara. . . .

[RAGUEL *puts a piece of Turkish delight into the mouth of* TOBIAS.

Thank you. I was saying, it's about Sara.

RAGUEL. Ah, yes, yes. A nice girl. Domesticated and so on. She is the apple of my eye.

TOBIAS. She must be. Raguel, I want to marry Sara.

RAGUEL. Well, that's plump and plain, anyhow.

TOBIAS. Yes. I have always studied to be both plain and plump. What have you to say about it, eh ?

RAGUEL. It is a little unexpected. I mean, you hardly know each other. It is a great honour that she has found favour in your sight. I need not say how delighted I should be to see her comfortably married to a respectable young man. And I don't think there is any possibility that you will quarrel about the settlement. Only, as I say, it is rather sudden. And old Tobit did me many a good turn in the old days. . . .

TOBIAS. All the more reason why you should make his son happy.

RAGUEL. I know, I know. But it's only fair to tell you . . . Well, there are stories going about. Not too pleasant ones either. It is all superstition and old wives' tales, of course, and I should never mention them to you if you were not an old friend, in a way of speaking, and an enlightened, educated man like myself. You know these Persians. A pack of heathens. Believe anything.

TOBIAS. Go on.

RAGUEL (*to the girls*). You clear out now. I'll look after the guest. Look sharp. No loitering.

[*The girls go.*

Have some grapes. Or a citron ? These pomegranates are very good. These nectarines are not bad. Home-grown. Yes. About Sara. Try a mango.

You know, my lad, the poor girl has been the victim of an extraordinary series of coincidences. They *are* coincidences, of course, but they are none the less heart-breaking.

TOBIAS. Go on. I need not tell you this is very interesting to me.

RAGUEL. Well, to tell you the truth, she has been betrothed and even married before. To be absolutely frank, more than once.

TOBIAS. Seven times.

RAGUEL. So many as that? Let me see. Five times, at any rate. No. You are right. Seven times. Tragic. Awful. Most reputable, decent young fellows.

TOBIAS. What happened to them?

RAGUEL. Well, we don't exactly know. It's a frightful trial to poor Sara. It's not her fault. I don't know how she has survived it. But they say she has been so unfortunate as to be the object of admiration of one of their horrible heathen gods—the foul fiend . . . (*he whispers*) . . . Asmoday.

TOBIAS. Who?

RAGUEL. Asmoday. You and I don't believe in such things. They say he has a tail like a dragon and a foul breath. Nasty ideas. It is getting chilly. Shall we go in?

TOBIAS. No. Tell me more.

RAGUEL. It is a strange country this, with its great pink, snow-topped hills, and its thick, dark groves. Terrible things happen here. I wish we lived in a homely and quiet land, where there are no devils walking in great winds at night. What did you notice first when you came to Persia?

TOBIAS. That no birds sing there. There is hardly a sparrow.

RAGUEL. And in the dusty desert there are birds all the way. I have only heard one nightingale and one lark since I came here, forty years ago.

TOBIAS. That is very strange.

RAGUEL. It is very strange in a country all trees and fountains and running streams.

TOBIAS. I will take Sara away from here.

RAGUEL. Go away from here yourself, my son. Sara is still a maid, and will be so, alas! till she dies. Her seven husbands were murdered—strangled.

TOBIAS. How?

RAGUEL. I cannot tell. But every one of them was

strangled on his wedding night. My daughter looked each daybreak like one whose soul has been on a long journey. She remembered nothing.

TOBIAS. Ough! It is growing dark and cold.

[RAPHAEL, *without:* "Tobias!"

RAGUEL. What was that?

TOBIAS. It was Azarias calling me. Perhaps he has found my dog. Never mind, Raguel. Give me your daughter.

RAGUEL. No! No! No! Your father's only son. No!

TOBIAS. I have been fighting devils all the way East from the Tigris. What do I care for devils? I have one fear only—that I shall die away from your daughter, as I *shall* die if you will not give her to me. I will die with her gladly. Go and tell her.

RAGUEL. Tobias!

TOBIAS Go and tell her. Send her to me.

[RAGUEL *goes. It is growing dark.* TOBIAS *buries his face in the garments* SARA *has left on the seat. There is silence for a little.* TOBIAS *begins to shiver; to sneeze. He wraps the garment round his neck and draws himself together with his hands. His teeth chatter.*

TOBIAS. Oh dear! Oh dear! What have I been saying? This is what comes of boasting and blowing and bluffing. And I can't get out of this infernal garden. They'll shoot me if I try to escape now. Azarias! Azarias! Come and get me out of this!

[RAPHAEL *appears from the grove with the dog.*

RAPHAEL. Stop that noise. Pull yourself together. Try to pretend to be a man.

TOBIAS. It's all very well to say "Pull yourself together," Azarias. I'm all to pieces. I never felt so rotten in my life. Toby, Toby. Oh, poor dog, you are going to lose your master.

RAPHAEL. The dog is laughing at you.

TOBIAS. Well, he ought to be ashamed of himself. It's no laughing matter. Do you know what I've done?

RAPHAEL. What have you done?

TOBIAS. I've offered to marry Sara.

RAPHAEL. Don't you want to marry Sara?

TOBIAS. Of course I do. Anyone would. But you know what happens to anyone who marries Sara?

RAPHAEL. Yes. And so did you. You should have thought of that sooner.

TOBIAS. But to be strangled by a demon. And oh, what a nasty demon, too. Azarias, get me out of this. You can marry Sara yourself, anything. Oh, Azarias, I'll give you half Gabael's ten talents if you get me out of this. Fifteen hundred shekels I'll give you, Azarias.

RAPHAEL. What a way to behave before your dog! You are a god to your dog. What must he think of you? You will make an atheist of him.

TOBIAS. Azarias, they will be back in a minute. What am I to do? What am I to do?

RAPHAEL. You are to marry the girl, of course. You want to. You ought to. You have got to. You can't run away now.

TOBIAS. But if Asmoday comes! A great fiend with a horrid breath!

RAPHAEL. I've no patience with you. Here, here's your pack. Take out the liver you took from the Tigris mud-fish.

TOBIAS. Oh, Azarias . . .

RAPHAEL. Be quick. Have you got it?

TOBIAS. Yes. Yes. It is all dry and tough like a bit of leather.

RAPHAEL. Slip it into the bosom of your djibbah.

TOBIAS. Why?

RAPHAEL. Don't keep asking me why. When you go to the ante-room of the bridal chamber, you will find a gold incense dish on a brazier. You will put that dirty bit of liver down on the gold dish of incense. You will put a lighted candle to the liver and it will begin to smoulder. There will then arise a nasty smoke and stench.

TOBIAS. But . . .

RAPHAEL. Hold your tongue. I rather think that will settle our friend Asmoday. He never washes, but he is a sensitive demon. (*He laughs.*) In the old days before the Fall, they had a nickname for him in the College of Cherubin. Do you know what it was?

TOBIAS. No, Azarias.

RAPHAEL. They nicknamed him the Stinker.

TOBIAS. And you think, Azarias . . . ?

RAPHAEL. It is vulgar of them, but we were—they were a mixed lot in those days—before the Fall. Good-night to you, Tobias.

TOBIAS. Don't go. Don't leave me.

RAPHAEL. I shan't be far away. I rather want to see Asmoday's face.

TOBIAS. So do I not.

RAPHAEL. I don't expect he'll bother about you at all. But he'll wonder who put you up to it. Now be a good boy and try to be a credit to me. I wouldn't do all this for everybody. It's a schoolboy sort of trick for a—for Azarias to play. Good luck to you, sonny.

Sings: " Aligor, Halphas, Belial, Belphegor
Went for a sail in a washerwife's tub.
They whistled old Glasya Labolas for a wind,
And they left Asmodeus in a quay-side pub.
Hey diddle diddle and a rub-a-dub-dub,
They went for a sail in a tub.

[*He goes off singing; in high good-humour. The moon rises.*

TOBIAS (*to his dog*). It's all very well for him, Toby. It looks to me as if he were too free with his talk of devils. He must have done himself pretty well in the servants' hall. But I suppose we'll have to go through with it, old dog. No way out now.

[*He reaches for the wine-bottle and helps himself to a good swig.*

Well, that's a help, anyhow. I don't know if daddy would approve, but I'll have another.

[*He has another. A nightingale is heard.*

By gum! There's the nightingale. The second ever heard in Persia. Perhaps things aren't so bad after all, doggie. And Sara is really a most charming girl.

[*A sound of stringed instruments is heard from the house.* RAGUEL *comes out, leading* SARA *in a bridal dress.* SHERAH, AZORAH *and two or three other girls follow; last of all* SAM, *the Æthiopian, with rich raiment for* TOBIAS. TOBIAS *rises as the head of the procession appears.*

RAGUEL. Sam, offer the Lord Tobias his wedding garment.

[SAM *drapes* TOBIAS *in the finery.*

Sherah, Azorah, light the torches.

[*They do so.*

RAGUEL. Tobias, it is meet that you should marry my daughter. Eat, drink and be merry.

TOBIAS. Father, you have an unfortunate way of putting things. At the moment I have no appetite. If you don't mind we shall have the marriage contract first.

RAGUEL. Very well. As you wish it. Take her then from henceforth according to the manner, for you are her cousin and she is yours; and the merciful Jahveh give you good success in all things. Sara, give me your hand. (*To* TOBIAS.) Behold, take her after the law of Moses and lead her away unto thy father. My blessings on you both. And now here is the instrument of covenants, we shall go in and sign it presently. Sara, my child, be of good comfort. It may all turn out well—quite well. Don't cry. We shall eat, drink and . . .

Never mind. For the present let us make the best of it.

TOBIAS. Do you know, I don't think Sara is very keen on the wedding feast either. Do you mind having it yourselves? A wedding feast is always rather trying, and when it comes to the eighth, and considering the circumstances—I think she would rather enjoy the cool night air for a little. Eh? What do you think, Sara?

SARA (*nods*).

RAGUEL. But the settlement?

TOBIAS. Oh, to Tophet with the settlement! Don't you realise . . . Here, give me the pen.

[*He signs the settlement and throws it back to* RAGUEL.

RAGUEL. But this is hardly business, is it? And where is Azarias?

TOBIAS. Raguel, in two minutes I shall go mad and bite everybody. Go to your dinner. I shall be in presently.

RAGUEL. Well, well. Very well. Your room is ready. One gets used to these nervous young bridegrooms. Come in everybody. Dinner is served. Dinner is served. It is hardly the way I like to do things, but I suppose it is all for the best.

[*All go out except* TOBIAS *and* SARA. *The music becomes a little more distant, but continues through their scene, reinforced by occasional bursts from the nightingale.*

SARA. What a nice little dog.

TOBIAS. Would you like him? I will give him to you.

SARA. Oh, very, very much. He will remind me of you.

TOBIAS. Sara, I must say you are the most tactless family I ever met. Just when I was beginning to forget.

SARA. Forget! It is easy for you to forget.

TOBIAS. Oh, is it! "Remind you of me!" Do you think I enjoy the prospect of having my life choked out by a filthy demon?

SARA. It's only once for you and then it's all over.

But for me it is again and again and again. How can you make me talk of such horrors?

TOBIAS. Sara, don't cry. It is pleasant here in the garden. The past and the future are outside high walls. We needn't look over the walls—even if we could. Don't cry, Sara.

SARA. You must love me very much to face death for me.

TOBIAS. I love you very much, of course. But as for facing death, . . . I am perfectly certain I shouldn't have done that if Azarias hadn't put me up to it.

SARA. Then you wouldn't . . . ?

TOBIAS. I'm only a poor little worm, really. I like to think I could die for you. I probably should have become very, very ill if I had gone on to Rages and left you. If I had only seen your eyes looking over your yashmak I should have remembered them for ever and pined away with longing. And Jahveh was kinder and more cruel to me than that. As I told Azarias, my knee-caps turned to jelly. . . .

SARA. Will Azarias stay with us when we are married?

TOBIAS. He certainly will not. Azarias is a very decent fellow and I don't know what I should have done without him. But I shouldn't like to be anchored to him all my life. He has a strong personality.

SARA. Yes. He has, hasn't he?—Oh!

TOBIAS. What is it, my lovely one?

SARA. I said " When we are married " as if we had years and years of life in front of us. Oh, go away. Go now before it is too late.

TOBIAS. But I love you, Sara.

SARA. I love you too, Tobias. That is why this time is worse than ever before. If I could die too I would be happy. But I can't die. Go away, my darling.

TOBIAS. I can't go now. Sara, it may not be so bad. Asmoday may not come.

SARA. He will. He will come. More surely to-night

than any other night—for I see happiness blazing up before me to-night. Asmoday will not allow me happiness.

TOBIAS. Oh! To Eblis with Asmoday! Look here, Sara. There is a chance.

SARA. There is no chance. Oh, sorrow continual! Oh, undying pain!

TOBIAS. Shut up and listen. Azarias has given me a charm.

SARA. Azarias? What is it?

TOBIAS. It is a charm he says will exorcise Asmoday. Personally I don't for a moment think it will. My own feeling is that Azarias was drunk to-night.

SARA. He wasn't. He couldn't be. Tobias, if Azarias gave you a charm it will work.

TOBIAS. Well, drunk or sober, joke or earnest, he has never let me down before.

SARA. How long have you known Azarias?

TOBIAS. Oh, we're old friends. Well, not exactly that. My father hired him for a drachma a day. He was well recommended by cousin Achiacharus.

SARA. But he gave you a charm?

TOBIAS. Yes. He did.

SARA. Then we are safe.

TOBIAS. Oh, do you think so?

SARA. He said we were safe?

TOBIAS. More or less, yes.

SARA. Didn't you believe him?

TOBIAS. Not particularly. He has peculiar ways of putting things. He probably just tried to cheer me up because he thought I ought to marry you.

SARA. He thought so?

TOBIAS. Yes; the unscrupulous devil.

SARA. Tobias. You are a brave little man. You are much braver than you think you are.

TOBIAS. Oh my beautiful! What do I care whether I die or not?

[*Silence.*

SARA. Let us go in.

TOBIAS. It is too soon. Couldn't we stay here?

SARA. Will the cantrip work here?

TOBIAS. No, it won't. No. That's true, it won't. (*A blast of wind is heard.*) What was that?

SARA. It was the wind.

TOBIAS. I don't half like it.

SARA. It is early for Asmoday.

TOBIAS. Coo! Asmoday! Let us go in! Hurry!

[*They go in. The wind howls nearer and then appears to recede. Music from the house. A light appears in an upper window. Enter* SHERAH *and* AZORAH. *They begin to put out the torches. The music dies.*

AZORAH. Well. There goes another.

SHERAH. Poor little man!

AZORAH. Little fool! He might have seen how smart we all were with the wedding ceremony. Practice makes perfect.

SHERAH. He must be very much in love with her.

AZORAH. Love is madness. Look at bad old Astaroth up there beaming as if butter wouldn't melt in her mouth. She knows! I would rather be bitten by a mad jackal than fall in love.

SHERAH. Well, I don't think it's fair.

AZORAH. What *is* fair? We are living in a game played by malignant fiends. And there are no rules.

SHERAH. I hope *one* malignant fiend comes and goes quietly to-night. I shan't be able to sleep a wink.

AZORAH. Woof! It is getting colder and colder.

SHERAH. That big valet of Tobias' is a fine-looking fellow.

AZORAH. Handsome is as handsome does. He looks at nobody. His blood is made of skim-milk.

SHERAH. At any rate I am glad Asmoday is not going to strangle him. But I am sorry for the little fat man too.

AZORAH. You are never happier than when you are snivelling. [*Puts out the last light.*

SHERAH. Oh, why did you put out the last taper? I'm frightened.

AZORAH. You needn't be afraid of evil spirits. You have no bones to crunch. Who's that?

SHERAH. Oh, Azorah!

AZORAH. Be quiet.

[RAGUEL *steals past with a pick and a mattock and disappears into the grove.*

AZORAH. It is only old Raguel with his pick and his mattock.

SHERAH Where is he going?

AZORAH. He is going to dig a grave for his latest son-in-law. He loses no time now. Let us go in. I am not afraid, but it isn't wise to be out when the Lord Asmoday comes for his nightcap.

SHERAH. What do you mean by his nightcap?

AZORAH. His evening hot drink.

SHERAH. And what is his drink?

AZORAH. Blood.

SHERAH. Oh, Azorah, come in. Come in, Azorah.

[*They go in.* RAPHAEL *appears in the grove. He wears the golden armour and great wings of an Archangel. He gazes at the lighted window. The wind howls dismally and there is a rumble of thunder.*

NOTE.—*At this point, if it is desired, the following Pantomime may be played. If not, and the Pantomime is not necessary to the action, the Curtain falls here on Scene* I.

PANTOMIME

(*Played by* RAPHAEL *and the Demon* ASMODEUS.)

The thunder grows nearer. There is a flash of lightning followed by a terrifying peal. A flickering green light from behind the wall illumines the whole back cloth. The Demon ASMODAY *appears, running along the wall on all-fours like a great tom-cat. He has a dragon's head with ram's horns and a great fish tail. He stands up to his full height opposite the window and makes triumphant and threatening gestures. A whiff of smoke comes from the window.* ASMODAY *draws back and registers baffled rage and disgust. He makes two or three more advances on the window, drawing back each time. Coughing and spluttering he staggers to* RAPHAEL'S *feet.*

ASMODAY. Who's there?

RAPHAEL. Good evening, Stinker.

ASMODAY. What?

RAPHAEL. I said, "Good evening." The correct answer is to repeat the phrase, not to stand there saying "What."

ASMODAY. Who are you? Are you Sara's eighth lover?

RAPHAEL. That is none of your business. You have been repeatedly warned to mind your own business, but there seems to be no curing you.

ASMODAY. What did you say just now?

RAPHAEL. I said "Good evening."

ASMODAY. You said something else.

RAPHAEL. Did I? Oh, yes. I called you Stinker. You are old Stinker Asmoday, aren't you?

ASMODAY. Who taught you that smoke magic?

RAPHAEL. Don't you know me, Stinker? Don't you remember the College of Cherubim? Look at me, Asmoday!

[*A blaze of light reveals the Great Archangel in golden armour, his huge wings spread.* ASMODAY *shrieks in terror and leaps into the green light.* RAPHAEL *spreads his wings and flies after him, uttering loud hunting cries.*

Darkness falls. After a moment's silence the dawn light begins gradually to grow. A nightingale sings.

SCENE II

Early morning in RAGUEL'S *garden. As the light thickens a lark begins to sing. The garden is empty.* SARA *and* TOBIAS *appear at the window. They lean out. They are dressed as on the previous evening.*

TOBIAS. What a delicious morning.

SARA. That is Persian air. Do you like it?

TOBIAS. By Gum! I do. I say, shall we go out.

SARA. Yes, rather.

TOBIAS. That's a lark singing.

SARA. I have never heard one before.

TOBIAS. We have them in Nineveh. The foul brutes of noblemen there eat larks' tongues.

SARA. Horrible. They deserve to live in Nineveh. Shall we go down?

TOBIAS. Come along.

[*They disappear.* RAGUEL *enters from the grove with his mattock and pick. He looks very tired and worn. He stops to listen to the lark.* TOBIAS *and* SARA *are running out hand in hand.*

SARA. Hello, daddy; what have you been doing?

RAGUEL. Eh? Oh, digging, digging.

TOBIAS. Digging? It is early in the morning for gardening.

RAGUEL. Yes. I find it keeps me fit.

SARA. Fit! You are half dead! What were you digging? We must go and see.

RAGUEL. No. Don't go. I was digging a hole. I have filled it up again.

TOBIAS. What an extraordinary thing to do! What kind of a hole?

RAGUEL. A special kind of a hole. It doesn't matter.

SARA. Were you burying treasure or digging it up or what?

RAGUEL. Now, don't torment me with questions at this hour of the morning. I must put away my tools. I am very glad to see you, Tobias. Very glad indeed.

[*He goes in.*

TOBIAS. What a queer old gentleman, if you don't mind my saying so, Sara.

SARA. Perhaps he was digging up my dowry.

TOBIAS. He didn't seem to be carrying anything back.

SARA. No. That's true. Let's look what he has been digging.

TOBIAS. Yes. Let us.

SARA. No. Stop. I think I know what he has been digging. How funny!

TOBIAS. What has he been digging?

SARA. How lovely it is to get out of that horrible, dangerous room and away from that nasty bit of dry leather you insisted on burning. Why did you burn that leather, Tobias?

TOBIAS. It was a cantrip invented by Azarias. And a jolly good one too, I think. Why was your father digging?

SARA. Oh, Azarias! Where has *he* got to, I wonder?

TOBIAS. He's probably sound asleep still. Oh, Sara, it is charming to be alive.

SARA. I think I'm dreaming. Are you alive, Tobias?

TOBIAS. Yes, by Gum! (*He kisses her.*) What do you think of that? Alive all right, eh?

SARA. Oh, darling bridegroom! There is nothing dreadful left in life. . . . Tobias.

TOBIAS. Well?

SARA. I was quite right about Azarias, wasn't I?

TOBIAS. In what way?

SARA. I said we could trust him. I said his charm would work. Didn't I? Didn't I?

TOBIAS. Yes. You did.

SARA. I think Azarias is wonderful.

TOBIAS. Oh, shut up about Azarias.

SARA. I don't think that's very kind. After all, I owe him the life of my husband. It wouldn't be very flattering to you if I weren't grateful to Azarias. And if you are going to be rude and brutal on the first day of our honeymoon, I wonder very much what it is going to be like later on.

TOBIAS. Well, you keep on talking about Azarias, and I keep feeling afraid you will make me jealous, and jealousy's the most abominable feeling in the world.

SARA. I only said he was wonderful. And so he is.

TOBIAS. No, he is not particularly wonderful and he was only doing his job. If he knew the trick he would have done very wrong not to tell it me, especially when he is drawing a salary for looking after me.

SARA. I thought you were wonderful too, but now I think you are mean and petty and contemptible.

TOBIAS. Sara!

SARA. You think of nobody but yourself.

TOBIAS. Well, honestly, I think that's pretty thick! By Gum, I do! Did Azarias run the risk of being strangled by Asmoday? No! Did Azarias terrify the bandit who attacked us on the road near Asshur? No! Did Azarias fight the devil-fish? No! Who did? I did. Azarias sat in perfect safety and gave good advice.

SARA. But it was good advice.

TOBIAS. For goodness' sake stick to the point—whatever it was—I forget now. You have upset me abominably.

[*He walks up and down.*

SARA. Tobias.

TOBIAS. What is it?

SARA. Don't walk up and down. Tobias, I'm sorry.

TOBIAS. Why sorry? I lost my temper. I should be sorry.

SARA. No, you shouldn't. I am a pig and you are my brave little hero.

TOBIAS. Of course I'm not a hero, but a man likes a little credit for what he has done.

SARA. You are. You are. You are a hero. I'm very, very proud of you.

TOBIAS. Are you really? I was beginning to be afraid you weren't. I should like you to be proud of me, Sara. I find it very difficult to be proud of myself. I have to keep lashing myself up to it. If you'll help me it will be quite easy to be proud of myself.

SARA. I'll help you, sweetheart.

[*They embrace.*

TOBIAS. Sara!

[RAPHAEL *enters. He is once more in his porter's disguise. He is as excited as his inherent dignity will allow him to be.*

RAPHAEL. Stop that a minute, Tobias. Tobias, I want to talk to you.

TOBIAS. Oh, good-morning, Azarias.

SARA. Oh, Azarias, your charm worked splendidly. There was only a thunderstorm and a great roaring round the house, and then Asmoday must have flown away.

RAPHAEL (*coldly*). Ah!

SARA. And we are so grateful to you, Azarias, my husband and I. I don't know where we should have been if it hadn't been for your forethought. I should have been a widow again.

RAPHAEL. Very probably. Tobias, I have had a magnificent night. Our friend didn't take long to realise that—that somebody of importance had a hand in the affair. Two or three seconds and you couldn't see him for smoke. He was quicker than I thought he would be. I went after him like a whirlwind and he climbed and banked and dived till I thought I should lose him. Over the Black Sea he took to the water, and it boiled and frizzled all round him. He nearly gave me the slip in the Caucasus first, but we had a straight burst across Anatolia and I got him just over the Nile delta. He was dead beat. Not an ounce of fight left in him. . . .

TOBIAS. Whatever are you talking about, Azarias? Have you been drinking again?

RAPHAEL. No. I have been dreaming. But it was a gorgeous dream. Pay no attention to what I said.

TOBIAS. You gave me quite a turn.

RAPHAEL. Asmoday won't bother you again. Call for me when you want me.

[*He goes.*

TOBIAS. What an extraordinary fellow! Great wits are very often to madness close allied, as Ezra said long ago.

SARA. I think you might ask him to be more respectful.

TOBIAS. Oh, we're practically friends. And I have a great deal to thank him for. Besides, he will be going back to Nineveh soon.

SARA. Aren't we going back to Nineveh?

TOBIAS. Yes, I suppose so. I have that bit of business to do in Rages first. With What's-his-name . . . Gabael. But that can wait. I am quite happy here. Aren't you?

SARA. Of course. I'm longing to see your father's place in Nineveh, of course. It must be so different—in a great city like that. Do you think he'll like me?

TOBIAS. He'll love you. He loves everybody.

SARA. How nice. Well, I had better go in. I must tidy myself up for breakfast.

TOBIAS. I am hungry too. . . . I say!

SARA. What's the matter?

TOBIAS. Where's Toby? It was breakfast made me think of him. What a shame! Poor old fellow!

[*He whistles.*

SARA. Don't mind him. The maids will be taking care of him.

TOBIAS. But he is so afraid of Djinns and Afreets. He may be half-way back to the Tigris by this time!

SARA. Unless you propose to run after him I don't know quite what you can do about it. Come in. (*Music is heard.*) Oh, how tiresome! Father is so punctilious. He must be dead tired, and there he has routed out the band for a hymn of thanksgiving. He can be maddeningly appropriate at times.

TOBIAS. Does he intend some sort of ceremony?

SARA. I suppose so.

TOBIAS. Oh, well.

[RAGUEL *appears in the doorway. With him* SHERAH, AZORAH, SAM *the Æthiopian, and a handful of maidens.*

RAGUEL. My beloved son and daughter. It has pleased Jahveh in His infinite compassion to spare the life of you, my son. It is well that we should mark and solemnise the occasion in no uncertain fashion, by such a feast as has never been seen in Ecbatana. Expense, my son, shall be no object. And in that expense you and I shall share equally.

TOBIAS. Father.

RAGUEL. Well, my boy?

TOBIAS. You remember what I told you about the camels and so forth? As a matter of fact, I shall be extremely short of cash until the dowry becomes due.

RAGUEL. Um! I could advance you a proportion. But stop a bit. You were going to Rages to see Gabael?

TOBIAS. About a matter of forty talents.

RAGUEL. Splendid. Gabael shall come to the feast. I shall send a trotting camel this very morning. . . . But I was making a speech. Where was I?

SARA. Father, you are tired and poor little Tobias is hungry. Might you not make your speech after the wedding breakfast?

RAGUEL. The breakfast is ready. It shall be as you wish.

TOBIAS. And, by the way, has anyone seen my little dog?

AZORAH. He is safe, master. He slept under my bed. He was very frightened. He has had his breakfast.

TOBIAS. Thank God for that.

RAGUEL. Very well. Very well. We shall go in. Oh, the happy day! Oh, glorious promise of ten thousand morrows!

SHERAH. May I not sing my little song, master!

RAGUEL. Um! Well, I suppose you had better.

SHERAH'S SONG (*accompanied by cymbals and tabors*).

1. It is the season of leaves and sheaves of green corn and soft, light rains.
Gone, gone are the storms of sand and the beat of the heat and the thirst and decay,
For the Afreet is fled and lamed and tamed and prisoned and bound with chains,
And the vine springs and the wind brings wings and the delicate dulcimers play :
Farewell, Asmoday!

2. Fled are the years of tears and the fears that have hung down on our hearts like a pall.
Rats, tarantulas, blood-sucking bats and the evil black gnats are away;
With the terror that walks and the fright that bites in the night they have gone away all.
And the soft blue pigeons coo and the lovers kneel down in the dew to pray.
Farewell, Asmoday!

[*During* SHERAH'S *song*, TOBIAS *and* SARA *stand holding each other's hands and gazing at one another entranced.* RAGUEL *fidgets with his beard.* AZORAH *circles round them in a slow dance.*

CURTAIN.

END OF ACT II.

ACT III

SCENE I

A khan near Kifri on the road to Nineveh. The scene represents a great yellow mud wall with a gateway in it. Beside the Gateway RAPHAEL *is sitting playing with* TOBIAS' *dog.* SARA *comes through the gateway with an amphora balanced on her head. It is afternoon.*

SARA. Azarias! . . . What a fright you gave me.

RAPHAEL. You have finished your siesta very early, Sara.

SARA. I couldn't sleep. Tobias is asleep. I don't know how he can. It is so hot. This is a horrible country. I came out to the well to get some water for myself. It was more trouble to go to the other end of the Khan and waken my lazy sluts of maids. And I couldn't wake Tobias. Isn't it hot?

RAPHAEL. Yes, it is hot.

SARA. The sky is like brass. Persia was nicer than this. Why aren't you in the shade? This sun is dangerous.

RAPHAEL. I like it.

SARA. But it will give you heat stroke. It is dangerous to like such things.

RAPHAEL. It is dangerous to like anything too much.

SARA. Oh, do you think so! I can't think that way about things. If—when I like a thing or—or a person, I just let go and go down the wind. There is no other way of liking. It can't be always dangerous. . . . I suppose we move on again at sundown. I am sick of this journey.

RAPHAEL. Are you?

SARA. You don't seem to care much whether I am or not.

RAPHAEL. It is natural for an idle woman to tire of a journey.

SARA. You think that of me? You think I'm an idle woman. I'm not. I'm not. I am . . . but you care nothing what I am. I don't know what you think of all day.

RAPHAEL. I don't suppose you do.

SARA. You are the most lordly sort of servant I have ever seen. You seem to consider yourself too superior for your job. Have the camels been packed yet?

RAPHAEL. It wants nearly an hour till sundown. I shall see to the packing.

SARA. Shall we ever get to Nineveh?

RAPHAEL. In eight days' march, I hope.

SARA. What sort of place is Nineveh, really?

RAPHAEL. It is as you find it.

SARA. Why do you answer me like this? Why do you stare through me with your great compassionate blue eyes as if you hardly saw me? Can't you see that I am in hell?

RAPHAEL. Yes, I can see that.

SARA. Then you know why?

RAPHAEL. Yes, I know why.

SARA. Azarias, I shall die, I shall die. I love you. I love you. Touch me only, Azarias and I shall die of joy. Azarias . . .

RAPHAEL. Don't be a fool, Sara. Take my hand. Look at me.

SARA. I know what you will think of me, but I have no shame and no fear. Take me to the hills, Azarias—away from here. I will be your slave. My heart stopped beating long ago when I saw you first in the garden. I love you, Azarias. There is no help for me.

RAPHAEL. Stop babbling, woman, and look at me.

SARA. . . . Are you a god?

RAPHAEL. There is only one God. I am the Archangel Raphael.

SARA. Master!

[*She falls at his feet.*

RAPHAEL. Get up. Sit down by me. . . . What ails you at the husband I have given you?

SARA. Oh, he is a good little man, but so commonplace. There must be hundreds of little men like him.

RAPHAEL. There are very few, Sara.

SARA. He is mean about little things and he snores in his sleep. . . . Lord, I know I am an ungrateful girl. I know I have a husband in a million. But I am different from other girls. I have had a terrible life. I think it has made me mad. And even as a baby I was different. I had dreams. . . . I loved beauty—oh, grand absolute beauty. How can I be satisfied with less? . . . There *must* be something about me, Lord, there must, there must. Why did Asmoday single me out from all the girls in Persia?

RAPHAEL. There is no accounting for anybody's taste, and I must be pardoned from attempting to explain Asmoday's.

SARA. Lord, you cannot hurt me now. I have spoken with an Angel. I am speaking to one now.

RAPHAEL. An Archangel, if you please.

SARA. An Archangel. I suppose it is a dream. . . . I knew you in the garden. . . . "The water-maiden blushed when she saw the god. . . ."

RAPHAEL. What is going on in your mind, woman?

SARA. "The sons of God saw the daughters of men that they were fair."

RAPHAEL (*standing up*). Sara, you have the mind of a child and the instincts of an animal. You have a smooth, weak, meaningless face. When your face moves prettily it is play-acting. When it is moved by emotion it is ugly beyond speaking about. When you take off your shoes you walk like a duck. Your whole body is a compound of absurdities and irrelevances. Your only admirable feature is the magnificent impudence that impels you to make sheep's eyes at an Archangel six thousand years your senior.

SARA (*begins to weep, silently*).

RAPHAEL. Don't snivel. You can't hope to make any impression upon *me* by that wretched exercise.

SARA. Very well. I shall kill myself.

RAPHAEL. I begin to think it is the best thing you could do. And I am not speaking solely in the interests of Tobias.

SARA. You are a cruel monster.

RAPHAEL. Please remember to whom you are speaking.

SARA. As if I could forget. Oh, what shall I do? What shall I do?

RAPHAEL. Is that a rhetorical question or do you really want to know?

SARA. I know the gods take pleasure in jeering at poor mortals. What is there to know? Is there anywhere any hope?

RAPHAEL. Yes, Sara. There is hope.

SARA (*looking at him quickly*). Yes? Yes?

RAPHAEL (*clears his throat*).

SARA. Oh, don't preach to me now. I can't bear it.

RAPHAEL. I never preach. Behave yourself or I shall go away altogether.

SARA. I will behave myself, dear Raphael.

RAPHAEL. Very well then. Listen.

You may fall in love with a man's dæmon—indeed it is advisable and stimulating to do so, provided that, at the back of your mind, you remember that you are only falling in love in a Pickwickian sense.

SARA. I don't understand you.

RAPHAEL. I shall try to make myself clear.

A dæmon, spelt with an "a," is a creature by whose agency you write immortal verse, go great journeys, leap into bottomless chasms, fight dragons, starve in a garret. . . .

SARA. Strangle our husbands.

RAPHAEL. Yes. That too.

It is perhaps fortunate that dæmons are much too occupied to visit, or to concern themselves with, the bulk of mankind.

SARA. It is very fortunate.

RAPHAEL. When it is necessary to Jahveh's purpose they make contact, often with extremely disturbing results; for dæmons are not all equally expert and conscientious, and their material is not invariably well chosen. I could talk for a thousand years on the methods and the shortcomings of dæmons. It is only necessary to tell you how to behave when you meet a dæmon. And evidently it is very necessary indeed.

Foolish women, of whom you are one, fall in love with dæmons. Your excuse has been that a dæmon of the inferior sort has tormented you since you were a child. He made you impatient with common men. He is now bound and in Egypt. There is no longer any more any excuse for you.

SARA. But I am still impatient with common men.

RAPHAEL. You must cease to be so. Often, at odd times in the future, you will see me looking out of Tobias's eyes. But you must look the other way and busy yourself with your household tasks. For I have no pity for you.

You must study Tobias, and Tobias alone—his little oddities, his little bursts of friendliness, his gentleness, his follies. You must love him for those and for his little round fat body.

SARA. But how can I help loving his dæmon?

RAPHAEL. You cannot love what you cannot understand. Love what you understand and you will understand more and more till your life is so full that there will be no room for anything else—torturings and itchings and ambitions and shames.

SARA. Very well.

RAPHAEL. You will some day make a new Tobias all of your own and understand him from the beginning, and that will be easy and pleasant.

SARA. Until his dæmon comes along and takes him away from me.

RAPHAEL. Until his dæmon comes along.

SARA. So be it, then. Good-bye, Raphael.

RAPHAEL. You will tell Tobias nothing of all this?

SARA (*laughing*). You don't know everything after all! Good-bye, Raphael.

[*Enter* TOBIAS, *yawning.*

TOBIAS. Hello, Sara! I wondered where you had gone. By Gum! I am sleepy. It's quite late. We must get a move on. Where did you go?

SARA. I went out to draw water, but I met Azarias here and we began to talk of this and that.

TOBIAS. I see. I say, Azarias, that old she-camel in Pultu's troop is badly galled on the off wither. It's very annoying. She's carrying four of Gabael's brass treasure chests. Pultu is a fool. I wish you'd go and have a look at her. We can't have the poor brute carrying all that weight if she's not fit.

RAPHAEL. Very well. I'll see what I can do. . . . Woolloh, Woolloh, Woollooh! [1]

[*He goes.*

TOBIAS. He's really an invaluable fellow. You're quite right about him, Sara. I believe he'll have that old lady camel as right as rain in no time. What were you talking about, you two?

SARA. Oh, nothing much. He is quite an interesting fellow. We were lucky to get him for a drachma a day.

TOBIAS. And all found. Yes, I suppose so. I'll tell my father I've been very pleased with him. . . . Well, sweetheart, only eight days from home. How surprised the old people will be!

[1] A camel call.

SARA. Yes, won't they?

TOBIAS. Their poor little half-witted son, Tobias, back with a glorious bride, and five troops of camels and poods and poods of shekels, and dressed up fit to kill! Dear old things. It is—how long is it since I've seen them, Sara?

SARA. Let's see. It took you thirty days to get to Ecbatana.

TOBIAS. Then there were fourteen days for the wedding party. I say, I thought it would never stop. I had the most frightful indigestion. And then when old Gabael turned up with his trotting camels and insisted on beginning all over again. And when the time was up I could hardly get away.

SARA. Father is very hospitable.

TOBIAS. The old people must think I am dead. I am more than a week late. We lost time on the way out. I do hope they are all right.

SARA. Why should they not be?

TOBIAS. Well, one can't do a journey for nothing, and I took most of the reserves of food and all the spare money in the house.

SARA. But I thought your parents were very well off.

TOBIAS. I'm afraid you did. Sara, I hadn't the pluck to tell you. They are very poor indeed. Not now, of course. But we have no fine house in Nineveh. Only a wretched little hut.

SARA. I never heard the like of that!

TOBIAS. Yes, isn't it miserable? I know what you think of me now. I'll never forgive myself. I'm a miserable cowardly little whelp.

SARA. I've a good mind to go straight back to Ecbatana.

TOBIAS. I was afraid of that. Well, that finishes it. I've already had more happiness than I deserve. I'll get Azarias to detail four camels and part of the guard. I'm sorry. That's all I can say. I'm sorry. . . . Azarias!

SARA. Stop that. I want to talk to you.

TOBIAS. Is there anything more to be said? I know what you think of me. You are free. You may go.

SARA. What sort of woman do you think I am?

TOBIAS. I have told you a hundred times. I have no words to tell you now.

SARA. It runs in my memory that a certain little fat man rescued me from Asmoday.

TOBIAS. No, no. That was Azarias.

SARA. It was not Azarias. It was you. Look up. Don't be a fool.

TOBIAS. Sara!

SARA. Tobias!

TOBIAS. You're not going to leave me? Even if I live in a slum?

SARA. Even if you live in a ditch full of cactuses and scorpions.

TOBIAS. Even if I am a liar?

SARA. All men are liars. There is no choice.

TOBIAS. But I am a coward.

SARA. You are nothing of the sort. If you say so again you will begin to be a bore, and that is much more dreadful.

TOBIAS. Then you aren't going to leave me?

SARA. I am not going to leave you.

TOBIAS. I am very glad. But I don't know what you can see in me.

SARA. I can see two nice merry little humble eyes. Guileless eyes, like a friendly dog's. And you have two chubby cheeks like fresh apples. May I kiss them?

TOBIAS. I see no reason why you shouldn't and every reason why you should. Shall I tell you what you are like?

SARA. Yes, do.

TOBIAS. In the first place, your eyebrows are like two rainbows springing from that alabaster tower of Babylon, your nose. Your eyes are like two brown pigeons sheltering behind purple hibiscus petals. Your brow is like nothing I ever saw in my life before. . . .

[*They go in affectionately through the gate.*

CURTAIN.

SCENE II

Outside TOBIT'S *house in Nineveh. The hovel is built into a wall in a narrow lane. The lane opens into an irregular sort of street. A steep bank of rubble intersects the street, and beyond it the domes and minarets of Nineveh are seen vanishing into the heat haze. The time is morning.*

Under a little shelter of black woollen cloth ANNA *is busy mending some garment or other.* TOBIT *is in the doorway of his house leaning against a jamb.*

ANNA. Eighty-five days. Eighty-five days. He is dead, I tell you, he is dead.

TOBIT. He has been detained. All sorts of things may have happened. Poor Gabael may be dead or sick and there may be nobody to give him the money. If it is so I am very sorry.

ANNA. It isn't Gabael who is dead. It is Tobias. I know it. I know it. Do you think a mother doesn't know?

TOBIT. Go on with your work. You are getting all worked up. I know he is safe. Be quiet.

ANNA. Be quiet you. You are only trying to comfort me. I know you, Tobit. Soft words, always soft words. . . . Oh, Tobias, Tobias, my only son, the light of my eyes. Did I let you go, Tobias? Did I let you go? Oh, why did I let you go?

TOBIT. Anna, dearest, he is only a little time overdue. Anything may have happened.

ANNA. Yes, anything. He may be lying at the foot of a precipice broken and dead with no one to help him.

Far from his mother who would give her life for him—gladly, oh, how gladly!

TOBIT. I know you would, mother, but surely you can have faith in Jahveh and in our prayers?

ANNA. Jahveh! Jahveh allows steep precipices to be, and bloodthirsty robbers to be, and wolves and bears. My little son, my little son!

TOBIT. Anna, you are making yourself unhappy about nothing.

ANNA. Is it nothing to lose all that I have? Is it nothing that the rest of our lives should be all blackness and sorrow?

TOBIT. It does not matter at which end of our lives sorrow comes. The sorrow and the happiness cancel out.

ANNA. I cannot understand how you can stand there talking like a copy-book at the moment that your only son is being torn to pieces by wolves.

TOBIT. Do be reasonable, Anna. How do you know he is being torn to pieces by wolves?

ANNA. I am the seventh daughter of a seventh son. I know these things.

TOBIT. Then you didn't know he had fallen over a precipice?

ANNA. He has fallen over a precipice *and* been torn by wolves. Oh, unbearable grief!

TOBIT. Nothing of that sort could possibly happen to him. That fellow Azarias is a most reliable man. I took to him from the first. I had an instinctive confidence in him.

ANNA. You have an instinctive confidence in every cut-throat and pickpocket and garrotter in Nineveh. Your instinct is nothing. A woman's instinct is the thing. It cannot lie. It is never wrong. Oh, Tobias! Oh, little, little Tobias!

TOBIT. Woman, you will make me cry too, and all about nothing. Azarias——

ANNA. Azarias! Didn't you say yourself he was a nobleman in disguise? The first day they had gone I *felt* Tobias was in danger. I know now. On that day Azarias cut his throat and threw him into the Tigris. I know he did, I know he did.

TOBIT. Anna, if you would stop inventing deaths for our son and go again to the road end and look out for him it would be more to the point.

ANNA. What is the good of that? I have looked and looked day after day till my eyes have nearly fallen out. I know he will never come back.

TOBIT. I have no patience with you. I have been into the bazaar a hundred times. If he had been dead I should have heard.

ANNA. How would you have heard? He has died in Media, far, far away from home and on a cold hillside. Oh, unceasing misery. Oh, Tobias, my son, my son!

TOBIT. Anna, my darling.

ANNA. You are as hard as a flint to any but your beggars and your lepers and your worthless tramps. What do you care for your own flesh and blood?

TOBIT. I shall go into the house and pray for Tobias—and for you. You are not yourself to-day. You are possessed.

[*He goes in.* ANNA *weeps for a little. Gets up and looks off L., shading her eyes with both hands. She comes back impatiently and goes on with her work.*

ANNA. My boy! My strong, handsome, beautiful boy! My only comfort, my only hope. Gone for ever, for ever. I shall never see him again. Never again. Never again. Never, never, never.

[*She falls asleep from pure fatigue, hunger and grief.* TOBIAS *and* RAPHAEL *and the dog appear. They are hidden from* ANNA *by the angle of the wall. They are dressed as Arabs, with long black cloaks reaching to the ground.*

TOBIAS. Did you hear that?

RAPHAEL. Hush. Tobias, would you like to see another trick?

TOBIAS. Don't be a fool, Azarias. I must go to her. Perhaps my father is dead.

RAPHAEL. Would you like to see another trick?

TOBIAS. I am tired of your tricks. Why did you make me leave Sara behind at the camp? She took it very unkindly.

RAPHAEL. She will be here presently. Would you like to see another trick?

TOBIAS. No. I want to go to my mother.

RAPHAEL. Stay where you are. Would you like to see another trick?

TOBIAS. Oh, very much, if that is what you want me to answer.

RAPHAEL. Do you see this?

TOBIAS. Yes. It looks beastly. What is it?

RAPHAEL. It is the gall-bladder of the fish you killed in the Tigris.

TOBIAS. What fish? Oh, yes; I remember. So it is. Why did you keep that disgusting thing?

RAPHAEL. Because I thought it would come in handy. Would you like your father to see Sara?

TOBIAS. What do you mean? That's impossible. The poor old chap is blind.

RAPHAEL. I know that. Answer my question.

TOBIAS. What question?

RAPHAEL. Would you like him to see Sara?

TOBIAS. Dearly. But it's hopeless. He has been to all the horoscopists and surgeons and magicians from here to Jerusalem. They all say it is hopeless. It is cataract.

RAPHAEL. Take this gall-bladder in your hand, and when your father comes out to greet you, strike the gall into his eyes.

TOBIAS. Look here, Azarias, a joke is a joke, but please remember I am not the soft sort of half-wit who left Nineveh with you nearly three moons ago.

RAPHAEL. Yes, you are. Will you do as I tell you for the last time?

TOBIAS. Oh, well. If it's the last time . . .

RAPHAEL. It is the last time. I have other work to do. Take the thing. . . . Now go to your mother.

TOBIAS. She is asleep.

RAPHAEL. She hasn't eaten by day or slept by night for five days.

TOBIAS. Oh, poor mother!

[*He kisses her.*

ANNA. Tobias! Oh, my darling son—— Not dead! Not eaten!

TOBIAS. It's all right, mother. Here I am. Are you glad to see me, mother? I got the money all right. I'm afraid I took longer on the journey than I intended. How is father?

TOBIT (*from the house*). Tobias! Sonny, sonny!

[*He comes stumbling out of the house, trips in the doorway and is saved from falling by* TOBIAS.

TOBIT. Oh! You've hurt me! My eyes! How strong you've grown! What muscles! You great ox of a boy! Oh, my eyes! They're burning! Never mind, sonny. It wasn't your fault.

ANNA. What's the matter, old man?

[TOBIAS *and* ANNA *help* TOBIT *to the seat under the awning.*

TOBIT. It's my eyes. It's something Tobias had in his hand. It got into my eyes. They'll be better presently. How are you, sonny? Thank God you're back.

TOBIAS. How are you, father? Has everything been all right since I went away? Has Achiacharus . . .?

TOBIT. Get some water for my eyes, Anna. They are burning like live coals. Yes, sonny?

ANNA. All right, daddy. I'll get some.

[ANNA *finds that the chagul at the door is empty and runs down the lane with it to fill it at the well.*

TOBIT. Oh, about Achiacharus. Poor fellow, he's in prison just now. He will get out all right, but he was a little injudicious. A little injudicious. The King came back from Shusha full of great schemes. And your cousin is of an economical turn of mind. But one requires tact in dealing with kings. Oh, my eyes! I could tear them out!

TOBIAS. Father, what have I done? It was Azarias: he gave me some . . .

TOBIT. Never mind, never mind, they are better now, a little. So poor Achiacharus is under a cloud. Only for doing his duty, poor fellow. I wish I could help him.

TOBIAS. But what about you? Have you—have you had enough to eat?

TOBIT. Oh, yes. It was a little unfortunate, your mother was so upset by your going away that she couldn't go out to the offices, and I—well I, in point of fact, was forced to do a little begging. Your dog would have come in handy. [*He laughs.*] How is the little fellow?

TOBIAS. You had to beg? Oh, the wicked, ungrateful son that I am!

TOBIT. Fortunately I am not a very good beggar. I did not make much at it. We shall easily be able to pay it back. How is my old friend Gabael? Was it quite convenient for him to pay?

TOBIAS. Yes, yes. I'll tell you all about that. . . . You see . . .

TOBIT. I wish Anna would be quick. The eyes are burning again. Oh, oh, oh! What a baby I am! But really they are extraordinarily painful. I could tear them out.

[*He rubs his eyes vigorously.*

TOBIAS. Azarias! What have you done? Do something for him, quick! He's in pain.

TOBIT. No. . . . It's . . . It's all right. . . . I . . .

[*He looks at his hands, then at* TOBIAS.

Oh, praise the Lord, I can see. The curtains are drawn from my eyes. I can see. I can see. Oh, Tobias!

TOBIAS. Father!

[*They embrace.* ANNA *returns with the chagul.* TOBIT *dashes at her, makes her drop it, takes her hands and dances round and round.*

TOBIT. I can see, Anna! I can see! I can see Tobias! I can see you! What a beloved ugly old darling you are. Kiss me. What do you think of the Lord now, you mournful old crocodile? Who is that gentleman over there?

TOBIAS. That's Azarias, daddy.

TOBIT. Oh, God bless you, Azarias. You've brought my son back and my sight back and—— Oh, what a happy day!

ANNA. A happy day indeed. Sit down, you old fool, you'll dance yourself to death. You've nearly killed me. Sit down at once and get your breath.

[SARA *comes down the street while all this is going on.*

TOBIT. And here is a beautiful young lady. What a blessed sight a young lady is. Were you looking for anything, my dear?

SARA. I'm looking for . . .

TOBIAS. Daddy, this is my wife.

ANNA. Your what?

TOBIAS. My wife. Sara is her name.

ANNA. But you never told us.

TOBIAS. I hadn't time!

ANNA. Time! You men! A girl would have screamed, "Mother, I'm married," as soon as she came in sight.

TOBIT. Girls have no real modesty. You are very welcome, my dear. It is a strange thing for a new daughter to arrive with none of the usual preliminaries, but you are very welcome.

ANNA. You're welcome to me too.

TOBIAS. She's Raguel's daughter, father. Raguel of Ecbatana.

TOBIT. Oh, joyful news! Oh, illustrious hour. Old Raguel's daughter, Anna! Think of that.

ANNA. We are very sorry to have to welcome you to such a wretched hovel, Sara dear, but we have seen better days, and if Tobias has had the sense to make any decent arrangements we shall see better days again. But I'm ashamed to receive you here.

SARA. Not at all. Your little house looks wonderfully cosy. Everything is so new to me in this big city. I wanted to see you quite informally, and when Azarias and Tobias slunk off like cats so early in the morning, I thought I'd better follow them. I hate a fuss and I hope I'm in time to prevent it.

ANNA. You are a dear, sensible girl and I love you for that. You are just the girl for Tobias. He is even more unpractical than his poor silly old father. Come in, my dear, and take off your things. You must be tired after your long journey.

TOBIT. How is dear old Raguel? I have always meant to go and see him. I had a slight temporary affection of my eyes. Nothing much, but it prevented me travelling or undertaking any engagements for eight years or so. It seems a long time. Dear me, what a lovely girl you are!

ANNA. The poor girl must be ill with fatigue. And you keep asking her questions and not allowing her to answer them. I'm surprised at you.

TOBIT. Aha! Listen to that! I've surprised old Anna! After forty years. Never mind, I'll surprise more than Anna, now I can see my way about. Go in, my child. Don't mind what a daft old man says.

ANNA. That's quite true. You are daft.

[*She goes in with* SARA.

TOBIT (*rubbing his hands*). What a splendid day! It'll take weeks to realise the splendour of it. Jahveh has made me a very happy man. Jahveh is full of unexpected moments. Look here, I am terribly sorry, but there isn't a bite to eat in the house, and you two boys must be starving.

TOBIAS. Oh, Azarias never seems to eat at all and I'm too excited to eat. It is beautiful to see you, daddy.

TOBIT. Oh, Azarias. You haven't quarrelled on the journey?

TOBIAS. Azarias has been a sort of a guardian angel to me, daddy. First he made me kill a devil-fish that was trying to kill me; then he made me terrify a bandit who was terrifying me; and he made me jump over crevasses I was frightened to jump; and climb cliffs I was afraid to climb; and walk distances I never thought I could walk. . . . Oh, and hundreds of things. And he made me look over Raguel's wall when I was afraid of the guards, so that I saw Sara like a water-lily in the morning. And Sara was bewitched by an enormous great fiend, but he made me marry her, although I was afraid of the fiend, and he told me how to scare the fiend away, and he went with Raguel's messages to Gabael and brought Gabael back, and he made me drive a bargain that took Gabael's breath away and made him shake me reverently by the hand. . . . And he hurried me back to you and taught me how to cure your blindness, and here we are.

TOBIT. And all for one drachma a day. What an invaluable man! You remember what I told you. Have you paid him regularly?

[TOBIT *and* TOBIAS *have walked to the bank of rubble. They sit down there, talking.* RAPHAEL *stays near the shelter.*

TOBIAS. Well. As a matter of fact . . .

TOBIT. Oh, Tobias! That's dreadful.

TOBIAS. I hardly liked to . . . I mean, one drachma a day to a superior chap like Azarias. No, I was proposing to divide the dowry with him. I think he has earned it.

TOBIT. I think he has. And he shall have five of Gabael's ten talents.

TOBIAS. They are eighteen now, daddy.

TOBIT. Eighteen! Tobias!

TOBIAS. Well, Gabael was quite pleased. Raguel said he got off very lightly.

TOBIT. Well, well. Perhaps it is all right. At least we must tell Azarias at once What will he think of you? He will think you have forgotten all about him. Azarias! Come here.

[AZARIAS *approaches the rubble bank and stands between* TOBIT *and* TOBIAS. *When he begins to speak he begins to climb the bank, and delivers most of his speech from the level of their heads.*

TOBIT. Azarias, we are grateful to the Lord for His bounty, but we must not forget you. Tobias and I have laid our heads together, and we have decided, as a small earnest of the great debt we owe you . . .

RAPHAEL. You owe me nothing.

TOBIT. I beg your pardon?

RAPHAEL. You owe me nothing.

TOBIT. Well, if you put it that way, it's exceedingly generous and charming of you to say so, but in that case perhaps you will be kind enough to accept a little gift as a token of our esteem and affection. We were thinking of . . .

RAPHAEL. I accept no gifts.

[ANNA *and* SARA *appear at the door.*

TOBIT. But, Azarias, it is good to give and to receive gifts.

RAPHAEL. It is good to praise Jahveh and to exalt His name.
It is good to keep close the secret of a king; but it is honourable to reveal the works of God.
I shall keep close nothing from you.
Tobit, a few prayers with alms and righteousness are better than many with unrighteousness and avarice.
Jahveh has heard your prayers and has seen your deeds that were themselves prayers.

[*He throws off his cloak.*

I am Raphael, one of the seven angels, who present the prayers of the Saints before the throne and who go in and out of the courts of Heaven.

Fear not, Tobit and Tobias, for it shall go well with you; praise God therefore.

I am not Azarias; I cannot eat and drink and walk the earth with you; I am less than a breath.

You have seen a vision.

Now, therefore, give God thanks; for I go unto Him that sent me.

But write all these things which are done in a book.

[*There is a blinding flash and a chord of stage music, and when* TOBIT *and* TOBIAS *have recovered themselves* RAPHAEL *has disappeared.*

ANNA. Lord have mercy!

TOBIAS. No wonder Toby was frightened. Do you remember, father, he was frightened to come in when the Angel was in the house? Do you remember? Poor little dog! And in Ecbatana again. And, Sara! I believe you knew all the time. Weren't you afraid?

SARA. Yes. But I grew less and less afraid of him, and he seemed to dwindle and fade till I could hardly be sure he was there at all. Do you remember at the gate of the Khan at Kifri? I saw him pale, like a ghost, and when he walked in front of you I saw you through his body. To-day I saw him like a drifting mist.

TOBIT. We have been visited.

CURTAIN.

END OF THE PLAY.

NOTES

PAGE *Author's Note*

vii *Jacobean phraseology:* the language-style of the English Authorized Version of the Bible translated in 1611 in the reign of James (Latin, *Jacobus*) the First.

Swift: Jonathan Swift (1667–1745), author of *Gulliver's Travels* (1726) and numerous other satires in prose and verse. His prose is a model of straightforwardness and clarity.

Arnold Bennett: (1867–1931), English novelist; author of *The Old Wives' Tale* (1908) and many other works of fiction. He wrote plain unornamented prose.

Tristan: the hero of the medieval love-romance *Tristan and Isolde*, now best known through Wagner's opera with the same title, first performed in Munich in 1865.

that . . . she should accept the inevitable: she had to be content with Tobit, the ordinary man, as a husband, since Raphael, being an archangel and not a romantic human hero, was not marriageable.

time had no objective reality: as a supernatural creature existing in Eternity, Raphael was not bound by Time, which is only a human conventional measure of duration.

Plato's dialogues: a series of conversational discussions of political, philosophical and other subjects by the great philosopher of ancient Greece, Plato (?427–?347 B.C.). Socrates is the principal speaker in the dialogues, the chief of which is the *Republic*.

detachment: avoidance of becoming emotionally or otherwise involved in affairs in which one is not intimately and personally concerned.

Afreet: a demon or evil spirit in Moslem (Mohammedan) mythology.

Reginald Scott: (1538?–99) author of *The Discoverie of Witchcraft* (1584), a work intended to discourage the persecution of those supposed to be witches. He was also an M.P. and wrote the first English book of instructions for growing hops.

---

xxvii *Ahasuerus:* the name given in the Old Testament (Book of Esther) to Xerxes I, king of Persia for twenty years before he was killed in 465 B.C. by one of his own soldiers. He invaded Greece and had a number of successes until his navy was utterly defeated by the Greek fleet at Salamis in 480 B.C.

khan: an inn at which travellers in Persia and other countries in the Middle East could rest and eat.

NOTES

Act I, *Scene* I

1 *seven-branched candlestick:* a Jewish ceremonial article for use particularly on days of religious observance. It derives from the description of such a candlestick in the Temple in Exodus 25. 31ff. There six " branches " are mentioned, the stem or shaft having the holder for the central seventh candle.

spade beard: one square-trimmed at the bottom.

a sturdied sheep: one that staggers about through the effects of a tapeworm in the brain.

get my bearings: find my position in relation to my surroundings.

antenna: the centipede has, of course, two antennae (" feelers ") extending frontwards; Tobit's stick, extended before him as he moves, acts as a single antenna.

2 *gone wool-gathering:* become absent-minded. The phrase dates from at least as early as the middle of the sixteenth century, when the gathering of pieces of sheep's wool which had been torn out on hedges and bushes allowed the gatherer to think about other things while wandering along.

Leviathan Avenue: an imaginary address, but one such as a house-proud person would delight to use as an indication that he lived in a " good " (i.e. expensive) neighbourhood. *Leviathan* was originally the name given to a large sea-monster in the Old Testament (see Isaiah 27. 1, Job 41. 1, etc.), but it has come to be used generally as a synonym for " great " in respect of wealth or power as well as mere size. *Leviathan*, written in 1651 by the English philosopher Thomas Hobbes (1588–1679), is a treatise on political power and government.

Chaldean vases: in Chaldea, a region between the rivers Tigris and Euphrates, fine pottery was made.

I never quite got used to a houseful of slaves: Tobit was a meek person who could not assert himself and was consequently despised by servants.

cataract: a disease of the eyes in which an opaque film slowly forms and eventually causes blindness. It can now be cured by a surgical operation, but in ancient times any cure for it would have been regarded as a miracle.

act of God: any happening which cannot be caused or controlled or averted by human means.

3 *caper-sauce:* perhaps this flavouring addition to food was known in ancient times: it is made by soaking in vinegar the buds of a shrub found in Mediterranean countries.

religious convictions on the subject of pig: since they regard pigs as unclean animals, Jews are forbidden by religious law to eat pork, etc.

a dose of bastinado: a beating with a cane on the soles of the feet.

3 *a repartee:* a witty or otherwise effective reply.

scrubbing offices: this is an example of the kind of analogy that Bridie uses in order to sustain his principle of not using archaic language; "scrubbing offices" must therefore be read figuratively to signify whatever lowly work Anna had to take when they became poor (in the Book of Tobit she evidently took-in washing).

4 *humiliation is a splendid tonic:* this is a hard saying which is only sometimes true; poverty and other forms of humiliation *may* act as a moral tonic by strengthening character through trial and adversity, but in other instances the effect may be depressing and degrading.

she had terrible pains in the abdomen whenever I stayed out a little late: This is a sly satirical allusion to what is believed by some to be a trick played by wives who pretend to be ill when they wish to keep their husbands at home.

housemaid's knee: swelling and stiffness of the knee-joints caused by too much kneeling while scrubbing and polishing floors.

Pentecost: a Jewish feast fifty days after Passover, corresponding to the Christian Whitsun.

the King's accountant: the keeper of the royal treasury.

loafers: idlers; layabouts.

5 *a generation that had no nerves:* this phrase and the sentence which follows it are, as Tobit indicates in his reply, favourite excuses of the young in all generations.

pillage: looting; wholesale robbery during wartime or other calamity.

hackles: literally, the long feathers behind the neck of certain birds, but used figuratively (as here) of a state of fear or anger aroused in animals and human beings.

Djinn: (genie; jinn) in Moslem mythology a spirit with supernatural powers; in Arabian tales often represented as able to materialize in human shape to perform good or bad deeds.

6 *a porter:* in Eastern lands during olden times, when means of transport were extremely difficult, porters were indispensable as carriers of goods and sometimes as guides.

arrack: a native intoxicating drink prepared from fermented coconut milk.

My master has a great regard for you, sir: This is one of Raphael's touches of comedy and, for the audience, a piece of humorous *dramatic irony*, for they know what Tobit doesn't know; namely, that what Raphael really means is "God loves you."

I am a teetotaller: No doubt it must be supposed that archangels and angels refrain from whatever may be considered bad habits, such as drinking intoxicating liquors. It must always be remembered, however, that in Bridie's play Raphael has a keen sense of humour and

6 enjoys making any remark that means more than it actually says or appears on the surface to mean.

water-skin: the skin of (usually) a goat sewn up to form a more or less water-tight bag. When hung in the hot tropical sunshine rapid evaporation keeps the water cool and refreshing.

chagul: native name for a water-skin.

7 *He wouldn't come in:* the dog Toby is aware by instinct of a strange Presence.

it is necessary to remember my poor co-religionists: Jewish religion and custom impose the rule that the poor must be cared for by those who are in better circumstances.

the bazaar: the native market which is a common feature of towns and settlements in the Middle East.

8 *take pot-luck:* (colloquial) be content with whatever food or entertainment is available when no special preparations have been made for guests.

garrotte: strangle; a method of murder by robbers or persecutors.

jackdaw: a bird that drops into hiding places objects it has collected.

die-hards: persons who never give-in until the very last moment.

9 *daft:* silly; stupid. But originally the word had an almost opposite meaning.

there is a Presence: Anna and the dog Toby are the only ones who have an immediate awareness of Raphael's superhumanness.

It is a pleasant rest to work in the Government offices: These words are put into Anna's mouth with a double intention. She speaks them quite seriously, but the audience will recognize in them the familiar joke that Civil Servants have an easy time. Bridie would not have been able to make this joke if he had made her take-in washing at home, as in the Book of Tobit.

Are you in Government employment, Porter? . . . Yes, in a sense: Another example of humorous dramatic irony. The audience will understand that Raphael is interpreting the question in his own sense, different from Tobit's, as Government of the Universe, i.e., Divine government.

The Courts: . . . " of Heaven " is implied.

10 *pi-dogs:* pariah dogs; scavengers.

bury him in the morning: the several references in the play to burial customs relate to important matters of Eastern ritual. Burial at times appointed by religious doctrine was a solemn duty; while any refusal by a tyrannical power to allow burial was a sin to be opposed by every means even if the punishment for opposition was death. The most impressive treatment of this problem in dramatic literature is in *Antigone* by the ancient Greek tragic poet Sophocles. It is one of the world's greatest plays, and English translations can be had (one is by Gilbert Murray).

12 *kid:* young goat.

sconce: wall-bracket.

you are too old to receive presents: he thinks that presents would only be given to young and pretty women.

scum . . . riff-raff: dirty disreputable people: but to Tobit none were " common or unclean ".

atheistical: unbelieving; irreligious.

13 *prig:* a smug, self-satisfied person.

Peloponnesian: a native of Peloponnesus, the large peninsula forming the southern part of Greece.

prickly heat: an irritating skin-rash which occasionally affects people in hot climates.

parchments: animal skins used as writing material before the introduction of paper.

14 *talents:* a talent was an ancient reckoning of money, the value of which varied from place to place: in Greece a talent represented roughly about £250.

note of hand: a signed promise to repay a loan.

shekel: a Jewish silver coin, or a weight of money.

a dirty usurer: although moneylending was common among the Jews, they hated *usury*, i.e., lending at excessive rates of interest.

bank rate: the modern term for the rate of interest on money lent by banks: the use of the term here is an intentional anachronism.

15 *spikenard . . . frankincense . . . musk:* an oil or ointment made from a fragrant herb . . . an aromatic gum used in incense burners . . . a glandular secretion of a particular species of deer.

money does not stink: This is an English version of the Latin *Pecunia non olet*, said by Vespasian (Roman emperor from A.D. 69 to 79) to his son Titus. He was expressing his cynical opinion that money carries no moral taint, even if it is acquired by disgraceful or questionable means.

foam at the mouth: now a colloquial expression for a state of extreme anger; originally the reference was to a kind of fit or apoplectic seizure which caused foaming at the mouth.

forty days' march: at, probably, an approximate average of ten miles a day, since they had to cross difficult country and mountains.

16 *an Angel in the house:* this phrase may have been an echo in Bridie's mind of a long poem by an English Victorian poet Coventry Patmore (1823–96), *The Angel in the House.*

says grace: offers a short prayer of thanksgiving for food about to be eaten.

pours a little water on the hands . . .: a custom of ritual cleansing.

Jahveh: ancient Hebrew name for God.

17 *You were dangerous to her once:* i.e., at birth.

18 *Noe:* Noah.

Israel: a name for Jacob (the reputed ancestor of the Hebrew race) as well as for the Jewish nation and their country.

Will this make me sick in the stomach . . . ? Will the remembrance make me ashamed?

19 *harlot:* immoral woman.

doddering: shaking with the feebleness of old age.

Go with God: a variant of Goodbye (God be with you).

20 *caravan:* for safety's sake and other practical reasons long journeys across difficult country were usually made in companies of varying size with pack animals (usually camels) to carry food and goods. Such a company of travellers was called a *caravan.*

We should have to know . . . about your family: i.e., in order to decide whether he would be a suitable companion for Tobias. This also is an example of dramatic irony, for the audience will share with Raphael the joke of which Tobit is unconscious—the question whether an angel is fit company for a human being.

after eating my salt: to eat salt (i.e., to take food) at a person's table was regarded as a pledge that no harm would be done at any time to the host or his family.

21 *polygamists:* men who have more than one wife simultaneously; the word is sometimes also applied to women with more than one husband, though they should properly be called *polyandrists.*

Nephthalite: belonging to the tribe of Nephthali.

drachma: an ancient Greek coin.

22 *haggle:* bargain: try to beat down the price.

mooncalf: (colloquial) foolish person.

strike hands: a form of handshaking.

yattering and yammering: gossiping aimlessly.

23 *I will extol . . . Amen and Amen:* this passage is based on chapter 13, verses 7–18 of the Book of Tobit.

aureole: a halo or disc of golden light shown around the head of a sacred person.

Act I, *Scene* II

24 *My stomach is flopping about my ankles:* a sensation of heaviness and emptiness due to physical exhaustion; but the word *stomach* is used here in the common English way as a euphemism for *belly*, which is stupidly thought to be less elegant than *stomach*, though both are simply parts of the body and are in different places. The proper synonym for *belly* is *abdomen*, if the simpler word is shunned.

25 *a slight abnormality in the region of my shoulder-blades:* a humorous allusion to his wings.

25 *thingummy:* colloquial word for anything of which the speaker does not know or cannot remember the correct name or description.

Psoriasis: a disease which causes scaly red patches on the skin.

a cock-eyed cannibal: this is to be taken as a humorous term of abuse in no way related to its literal meaning of a cross-eyed eater of human flesh.

when we were camel-borne gentry: as a present-day equivalent, a person who was once wealthy might say " when we went about in a Rolls-Royce ".

It's like heaven with the lid off: a reversal of the common colloquial phrase ". . . like hell with the lid off " for anything terrifying.

fairway: a channel free from obstacles.

26 *By gum:* a colloquial substitute for the oath " By God . . ."

Jonas: Bridie found the story of Jonah (Jonas) and the whale in the Old Testament so fascinating that he wrote three versions of his own play *Jonah and the Whale.*

27 *gut the fish:* prepare it for cooking by taking out the inner parts.

at once a physiological and a philosophical problem: " physiological " in respect of its use to the fish while alive, " philosophical " in respect of the use Raphael has planned for it.

eyes like two full moons . . .: oriental literature makes much use of such extravagantly romantic poetical language, as can be seen, for example, in The Song of Solomon in the Old Testament.

papyrus lily: the flower of a water-plant which is depicted in ancient Egyptian paintings, and from which a kind of writing paper was made after the stalks had been beaten and dried.

horoscope: an estimate of a person's character and a forecast of his/her future, based upon information regarding the position of the planets at the time of his/her birth. The casting of horoscopes is a branch of astrology derived from the theory or superstition that the nature and destiny of each human being is influenced by the stars. The girl referred to here was supposed to be under the influence of the planet Mercury, aided by the other curious measures described.

28 *a woodcutter:* in many old stories it is a poor woodcutter's son who marries a king's daughter as the reward for some heroic deed or miraculous service.

a half-wit: this does not necessarily mean that he was mentally deficient, but rather that he was simple and guileless.

braxy ram: a male sheep suffering from a fatal disease of the spleen.

rehearsing: used here in the sense of " announcing ".

Kurdish: from Kurdistan.

Salaam aleikum: " May peace be upon you ": the customary Moslem greeting.

28 *the gentle pastime of angling:* fishing has long been called " the gentle craft ", since it is a quiet meditative pastime—though it probably seems otherwise to the fish.

29 *Jehudi:* the Arabic form of " Jew ".

sotto voce: (Italian: " beneath the voice ") under his breath; in an undertone.

rhetoric: in modern usage, public speaking in a high faluting style intended to impress the hearers, though the speaker may be insincere.

Gehannum: gehinnom, the Hebrew word for hell, the place of everlasting torment.

hairy-toed polecat . . . father of sixty dogs: oriental peoples have a much larger, more varied and more imaginative vocabulary of abuse than the British, who rarely go beyond the vulgar repetition of a bare half-dozen meaningless swear words.

30 *Your liver is too white:* there was an unfounded belief that the liver of a coward was bloodless and therefore white instead of red; hence the familiar term " lily-livered ".

Act II, *Scene* I

32 *arbutus:* a species of evergreen shrub.

zither: a flat, stringed musical instrument.

33 *a kitten in the temple at Thebes:* Thebes was a city on the lower Nile in ancient Egypt, a country where cats were regarded as sacred creatures.

Cadi: a town judge.

smokes from a feeding-bottle: a humorous reference to a *hookah* or *hubble-bubble*, a smoking device in which the tobacco burns in a vase from which the smoke passes through water before being drawn to the user's mouth through a flexible tube.

34 *make obeisance:* bow low.

He goggles: stares with wide-open fascinated eyes.

sugared gelatine: presumably the sweetmeat usually called " Turkish delight ".

Circassian: Circassia was a country bordering the north shore of the Black Sea; now Soviet provinces. Circassian women were famous for their exceptional beauty.

35 *Play the game:* (a familiar English phrase) play fairly: don't cheat.

making an exhibition of yourself: " showing off "; making yourself look foolish.

39 *waggish:* facetious; joking.

collation: in this sense, a meal (usually cold) served between the usual times for eating.

39 *Bonnie, Bonnie Banks of the Tigris:* Bridie gives her song this title in humorous allusion to the famous Scottish song " The Bonnie Banks of Loch Lomond. "

social welfare: a modern phrase, here intended to refer to charitable work among the poor .

40 *standoffish:* unsociable; disinclined to mix with other people.

broad-minded: having no fixed opinions or prejudices; tolerant.

cosmopolitanism: interest in and goodwill towards people of every nation; the opposite of nationalism.

a poor Highland girl with no civilization and no manners: Bridie was a Lowlander (i.e., a native of southern Scotland) and therefore enjoyed a sly joke at Highlanders (a familiar name for northern Scots).

41 *that screeching guinea-fowl:* her abusive term for Azorah (see page 35).

there is a god in the garden: Bridie probably intended this as an echo of an English poem by T. E. Brown (1830–97), " My Garden ", which begins " A garden is a lovesome thing, God wot!" and ends " 'Tis very sure God walks in mine." Though written seriously and taken seriously in the nineteenth century, it has in more recent years been laughed at by those who regard it as excessively pious and sentimental.

O my celestial ibis . . .: another example of the flowery oriental style; the *ibis* is a graceful long-legged bird treated as sacred in ancient Egypt; *jacinth* is a precious gem-stone, orangey-red in colour.

42 *She is much more beautiful . . .:* Though this speech is in the oriental style and spoken with lyrical seriousness by Tobias, it is largely a parody, for Sara would be a monster if she were truly represented by the imagery in these lines.

43 *Baal:* this Hebrew word meaning " Lord " applied to many local gods, though particularly to the Baal who failed his 450 prophets when they were challenged by Elijah (see the Old Testament, I Kings 18. 17–40).

44 *while they are washing his hands and feet:* for ritual cleansing.

the servants' hall: where the servants ate and congregated in their leisure time in English mansions. There is unlikely to have been a similar apartment in Raguel's house, but Bridie uses the familiar term to denote the servants' quarters, in whatever form.

apt to be familiar: inclined to regard themselves as social equals of the upper classes, instead of accepting the inferior position that was thought proper for them.

Domesticated: trained in household duties.

the apple of my eye: the centre of loving attention: in Deuteronomy 32. 10 it is said that the Lord kept Jacob " as the apple of his eye ". Before its structure was understood, the pupil of the eye was believed to be solid like an apple.

45 *plump and plain:* (idiom) downright and straightforward in speech and action. Tobias replies by using the words in their physical sense of " fat and ugly ".

the settlement: the marriage portion or dowry; the money or property settled on a girl by her father when she marries.

old wives' tales: made-up stories that should not be believed; of the kind supposed to have been put about by credulous old women or by witches. St. Paul wrote in his first epistle to Timothy (4. 7) " refuse . . . old wives' fables and exercise thyself rather unto godliness "

citron: a large lemon-shaped fruit.

47 *pretend to be a man:* show some manly courage.

48 *djibbah:* a long jacket.

brazier: a metal stand supporting a small charcoal fire.

49 *before the Fall:* i.e., before Adam and Eve disobeyed God's command (Genesis ch. 3).

Cherubin: one of the nine orders of heavenly angels; the College of Cherubin is, of course, imaginary.

a schoolboy sort of trick for a—: he almost betrays himself by saying " for an angel ", but stops just in time.

Aligor . . . for a sail in a tub: a made-up nonsense song; when Bridie wrote it he may have been remembering Edward Lear's " The Jumblies " who " went to sea in a sieve ".

50 *Eat, drink and be merry:* the ancient Egyptians used to remind themselves of the shortness of human life by saying at their feasts " Let us eat and drink, for tomorrow we die "; these words also occur in the Old Testament, Isaiah 22. 13; and Jesus in one of his parables spoke of the foolish rich man who said to his soul " take thine ease, eat, drink, and be merry ".

the instrument of covenants: the document fixing the amount of the marriage settlement.

51 *Tophet:* a place south of Jerusalem where corpses and refuse were thrown and a fire was kept constantly burning; the name came into use as a synonym for hell.

52 *yashmak:* a veil hiding all but the eyes; worn by Moslem women when in public.

pined away: wasted away.

53 *Eblis:* a fallen angel mentioned in the Koran.

54 *cantrip:* (Scottish) piece of witchcraft or mischief.

handsome is as handsome does: an English proverb meaning that good looks are useless without good nature and good deeds.

55 *mattock:* a kind of pickaxe with sharp-edged flattened ends, one parallel with the shaft, the other at right angles to it.

NOTES

Act II, *Scene* II

59 *that's pretty thick:* (colloquial) that is unfair. But the fun here is that everything Tobias claims credit for has in fact been done by Raphael.

61 *as Ezra said:* the many sayings of the prophet Ezra are recorded in the Book of Ezra in the Old Testament and in the two Books of Esdras (another form of Ezra) in the Apocrypha.

62 *punctilious:* strictly attentive to custom and ceremony.

maddeningly appropriate: so determined to do the "right thing" that he makes her angry.

a trotting camel: a camel used for fast riding, as distinct from a laden slower-moving one carrying goods.

63 *dulcimers:* stringed instruments somewhat resembling zithers, except that they are played by striking the strings with hammers, whereas the strings of zithers are plucked.

Act III, *Scene* I

64 *amphora:* a two-handled water vessel.

It is dangerous to like anything too much: Because of the suffering that its loss may bring.

go down the wind: to drift as circumstances dictate and not protest or struggle against what cannot be avoided.

65 *It is as you find it:* It depends upon how you look at it or feel about it.

66 *I am different from . . .:* This is a conceited person's way of claiming to be better than other people; another way of saying "I have an artistic temperament", which is usually a bogus claim.

The sons of God saw the daughters of men that they were fair: quoted from Genesis 6. 2.

you have the mind of a child . . .: This paragraph is Raphael's recipe for getting the romantic nonsense out of Sara.

67 *daemon:* genius; spiritual force.

in a Pickwickian sense: not in a common or usual sense (see chapter 1 of *Pickwick Papers* by Charles Dickens).

68 *Foolish women . . . fall in love with daemons:* women who fall in love with geniuses (artists, poets, musicians) often find that they lack the domestic virtues desirable in a husband and are irritable and inconsiderate. As Raphael says, "You cannot love what you cannot understand"; and, though no woman would admit it, women do not understand geniuses; they only try to "improve" them!

galled on the off wither: sore on the right-hand side of the ridge between the animal's shoulders.

as right as rain: (idiom) in good order. (Though this is a familiar saying the connection between rain and rightness is not obvious;

68 perhaps rain falling straight down at right angles to the ground originally suggested the phrase. More probably it was the accidental product of alliterative attraction—*r*ight as *r*ain.)

70 *poods:* a pood is a Russian measure of weight equal to 36 lb.

dressed up fit to kill: a familiar colloquial phrase of uncertain origin meaning elaborately dressed or correctly dressed for a formal occasion or celebration.

71 *All men are liars:* See Psalm 116. 11, " I said in my haste, All men are liars."

Act III, *Scene* II

72 *Do you think a mother doesn't know?:* Anna says later: " A woman's instinct is the thing." But it proves unreliable and thus gives support to those who declare that " women's instinct " is a myth originated to give them a sense of superiority over men, who are guided by evidence and reason.

76 *injudicious:* unwise.

78 *Girls have no real modesty:* In his autobiography *One Way of Living*, Bridie includes " A Lecture on Women " containing both humorous and serious comments and critical observations. Tobit's statement about girls was no doubt approved by the author!

79 *prevented me travelling:* " prevented my travelling " is grammatically correct.

81 *accept a little gift as a token of our esteem and affection:* an echo of the pompous formal language often used by English speakers when making a presentation.

It is good to praise Jahveh . . .: This passage is based on the Book of Tobit 12. 6–20.

82 *one of the seven angels:* the other six archangels are Michael, Gabriel, Uriel, Chamuel, Jophiel, and Zadkiel. Only Michael and Gabriel are named in the Authorized Version of the Bible; all are named in the Apocrypha (Book of Enoch). Raphael is the only one in the Book of Tobit.